Warrior Mindset: A Veteran's Guide to Entrepreneurship and Business

Dr. Jose A. Mendez

Published by Christian Cross Publishing LLC, 2024.

While every precaution has been taken in the preparation of this book, the publisher assumes no responsibility for errors or omissions, or for damages resulting from the use of the information contained herein.

WARRIOR MINDSET: A VETERAN'S GUIDE TO ENTREPRENEURSHIP AND BUSINESS

First edition. February 29, 2024.

ISBN: 979-8224009862

Written by Dr. Jose A. Mendez.

Table of Contents

DEDICATION

To my dear brothers and sisters of the Armed Forces,

This book is dedicated to you, the brave souls who have selflessly served in the armed forces. Your unwavering dedication, sacrifice, and courage have inspired me beyond words. As you embark on your entrepreneurial journey, may you carry with you the same resilience, determination, and sense of duty that you have demonstrated in service to our country. Remember that your experiences have equipped you with invaluable skills and perspectives that will undoubtedly guide you through the challenges of entrepreneurship. Your commitment to excellence and your willingness to overcome obstacles are testaments to your strength of character. I am honored to call you my brothers and sisters, and I have no doubt that you will achieve great success in all your endeavors.

To those who made the ultimate sacrifice,

May the memory of those who laid down their lives in defense of our country live forever in the history of our country. Your bravery, valor, and selflessness will never be forgotten. Though you are no longer with us, your legacy lives on in the freedoms we cherish and the opportunities we pursue. We honor your sacrifice by striving to build a better future, one filled with hope, prosperity, and peace. Your courage inspires us to persevere in the face of adversity and to cherish each moment we are given. May your memory be a source of strength and inspiration to all who read these pages. We salute you; we remember you, and we are forever grateful for your service and sacrifice.

With deepest gratitude and respect,

Dr. Jose A. Mendez

ACKNOWLEDGMENTS

FIRST AND FOREMOST, I extend my sincere appreciation to the team at Christian Cross Publishing for their unwavering support, dedication, and belief in the vision behind this project. Your commitment to excellence and passion for spreading inspirational Christian literature and Christian Authors have been instrumental in bringing this book to fruition.

I also want to extend my gratitude to the dedicated team at the printing and distribution facilities who have worked tirelessly to ensure that this book reaches readers around the world. Your professionalism and commitment to quality are deeply appreciated.

I am indebted to my family and friends for their unwavering support and encouragement throughout this journey. Your love, encouragement, and understanding have sustained me through the challenges and triumphs of the writing process.

Lastly, I extend my heartfelt thanks to the readers of Christian Cross Publishing for your support and enthusiasm for our mission of spreading the message of faith, hope, and love through literature. It is my honor and privilege to serve you, and I am deeply grateful for the opportunity to share this journey with you.

With sincere appreciation,

DR. JOSE A . MENDEZ

Warrior Mindset:

A Veteran's Guide to Entrepreneurship and Business

Chapter 1: The Warrior Mindset

The Military Mindset: A Foundation for Success

In the book "Warrior Mindset: A Veteran's Guide to Entrepreneurship and Business" we explore the powerful connection between military experience and entrepreneurial success. This subchapter, "The Military Mindset: A Foundation for Success," delves into the unique qualities and skills that veterans possess and how they can be harnessed to achieve remarkable results in the business world.

For general readers, this book offers valuable insights into the mindset of military personnel and the transferable skills they bring to the table. Understanding the military mindset can help foster empathy and appreciation for the challenges veterans face when transitioning into civilian life. Moreover, it provides a framework for individuals to adopt certain military principles in their own lives and careers, enhancing their chances of success.

Veterans reading this subchapter will find affirmation of their value in the business world. We delve into the attributes that make veterans exceptional entrepreneurs, such as discipline, adaptability, resilience, and the ability to work well under pressure. By recognizing and capitalizing on these strengths, veterans can find a sense of purpose and fulfillment in their entrepreneurial endeavors.

Business people will gain a fresh perspective on the advantages of hiring veterans or partnering with veteran-owned businesses. The military mindset brings a unique skill set and work ethic that can greatly benefit any organization. Moreover, this subchapter offers practical advice on how to tap into the potential of veteran employees and create a supportive environment that allows them to thrive.

For military personnel considering entrepreneurship, this subchapter serves as a roadmap for leveraging their military experience. We explore how to translate military skills into the business world, navigate the challenges of starting a business, and build a network of support. By embracing their military mindset and applying it to their entrepreneurial journey, veterans can find a new sense of purpose and create successful businesses that make a positive impact.

"The Military Mindset: A Foundation for Success" is a powerful book that sheds light on the unique qualities veterans bring to the business world. Whether you are a general reader, a veteran, a business person, or a military personnel, this chapter provides valuable insights and practical strategies to unleash your potential and achieve entrepreneurial success.

Discipline and Resilience

In the pursuit of entrepreneurship, the qualities of discipline and resilience are essential for success. These traits are particularly relevant to veterans transitioning into the world of business, as they have already honed these skills during their military service. The subchapter "Discipline and Resilience" delves into the importance of these qualities and provides practical strategies for harnessing them to achieve business success.

For veterans, discipline is ingrained in their DNA. It is the foundation upon which they have built their military careers, and it is this same discipline that can drive their entrepreneurial endeavors. In the business world, discipline manifests itself through consistent action, adherence to routines, and the ability to stay focused on long-term goals. This subchapter explores how veterans can leverage their military discipline and apply it to their business ventures, providing valuable insights and actionable steps to ensure sustained success.

Resilience, too, is a hallmark trait of veterans. The ability to bounce back from adversity, adapt to new environments, and overcome challenges is a testament to the resilience cultivated during their military service. This subchapter highlights the importance of resilience in entrepreneurship and provides veterans with strategies to navigate the inevitable obstacles they will encounter along the way. By drawing upon their military experiences, veterans can tap into their wellspring of resilience to persevere and thrive in the face of adversity.

"Discipline and Resilience" also addresses the unique perspectives and strengths that veterans bring to the business world. Their military background instills them with a strong work ethic, a keen sense of teamwork, and an unwavering commitment to excellence. Leveraging these qualities, veterans can differentiate themselves in the competitive landscape of entrepreneurship and forge their path to success.

Throughout this subchapter, veterans, businesspeople, and military personnel will find actionable advice, and real-life insights to help them cultivate discipline and resilience in their entrepreneurial journey. By embracing these qualities and harnessing their unique strengths, veterans can navigate the challenges of business ownership with confidence and achieve remarkable success.

In summary, "Discipline and Resilience" empowers veterans to leverage their military backgrounds in entrepreneurship. Through practical strategies, valuable insights, and real-life experience, this subchapter equips veterans with the tools they need to harness discipline and resilience for business success. Whether they are starting their own venture or joining an existing organization, veterans can tap into their warrior mindset to excel in the world of business.

Goal Setting and Mission Focus

Goal setting and mission focus are two key components that drive success and growth. These principles are particularly relevant to veterans transitioning into the realm of entrepreneurship. As veterans, you possess the discipline, determination, and resilience necessary to tackle any challenge that comes your way. By applying these skills to setting goals and staying focused on your mission, you can propel yourself to new heights of achievement in the business world.

Setting clear, achievable goals is the first step towards success. Goals provide direction and purpose, acting as a roadmap that guides your actions and decisions. When setting goals, it is important to make them specific, measurable, attainable, relevant, and time-bound (SMART). By following this framework, you set yourself up for success by having a clear vision of what you want to achieve and a plan to get there.

However, goal setting alone is not enough. Maintaining a laser-like focus on your mission is equally important. Your mission is the overarching purpose and vision that drives your business. It is the reason you wake up every morning and the force that keeps you going when faced with obstacles. By staying focused on your mission, you can align your actions and decisions with your long-term goals, ensuring that every step you take brings you closer to your vision.

For veterans, mission focus is already ingrained in your DNA. In the military, you were trained to prioritize the mission above personal interests, to adapt and overcome, and to remain focused even in the face of adversity. These qualities are invaluable in the world of entrepreneurship, where challenges and setbacks are inevitable. By harnessing your military experience and applying it to your business endeavors, you possess a unique advantage that sets you apart from others.

To maintain mission focus, it is essential to cultivate a mindset of resilience and determination. Embrace failures as learning opportunities and setbacks as temporary roadblocks. Stay committed to your mission, even when faced with doubts or setbacks. Surround yourself with a network of mentors, fellow veterans, and like-minded individuals who can support and motivate you along the way.

Goal setting and mission focus are vital for any entrepreneur, particularly for veterans transitioning into the business world. By setting clear, SMART goals and maintaining a laser-like focus on your mission, you can utilize your military experience to achieve extraordinary success. Remember, your training and experience have equipped you with the skills necessary to overcome any challenge and thrive as a veteran entrepreneur. Stay focused, stay determined, and let your warrior mindset guide you towards business success.

Teamwork and Leadership

In today's fast-paced and competitive business world, the importance of teamwork and leadership cannot be overstated. In this book we delve into the crucial aspects of teamwork and leadership, providing valuable insights and strategies for veterans, businesspeople, and military personnel alike.

As veterans, we are no strangers to the power of teamwork. Our military experiences have taught us the significance of working together towards a common goal, relying on the strengths and abilities of each team member. In the business world, this mindset is equally essential, and harnessing the power of effective teamwork can lead to unparalleled success.

One key aspect of teamwork is communication. Clear and concise communication allows team members to understand their roles and responsibilities, ensuring that everyone is on the same page. In this book we explore various communication techniques, including active listening and open dialogue, that can help foster a strong team dynamic.

In addition to communication, effective leadership plays a vital role in achieving business success. As veterans, we have experienced leadership in its purest form, and we understand that true leaders lead by example. In this subchapter, we delve into the qualities and characteristics of effective leaders, providing practical tips on how to inspire and motivate your team towards a shared vision.

Moreover, we understand that transitioning from the military to entrepreneurship can be a challenging journey. That's why we offer guidance on how to leverage your military experience and apply it to your entrepreneurial endeavors. The discipline, adaptability, and problem-solving skills honed in the military can be invaluable assets in the business world. We share inspiring stories of veteran entrepreneurs who have successfully navigated this transition, providing a roadmap for your own entrepreneurial journey.

Whether you are a veteran looking to start your own business or a business professional seeking to enhance your teamwork and leadership skills, "Warrior Mindset, Business Success" offers practical and actionable advice. By embracing the power of teamwork and cultivating effective leadership qualities, you can overcome obstacles, drive innovation, and achieve unparalleled success in your entrepreneurial pursuits.

Join us on this transformative journey of teamwork and leadership, as we unlock the full potential of your entrepreneurial spirit. Together, we can conquer challenges, overcome adversity, and create a legacy of success.

Transitioning from the Military to Entrepreneurship

The journey from military service to becoming a successful entrepreneur is not an easy one. It requires a unique mindset and a set of skills that many veterans already possess. In this subchapter, we will explore the challenges and opportunities that come with transitioning from the military to entrepreneurship, as well as provide guidance and advice to help veterans navigate this exciting path.

One of the biggest challenges veterans face when making the transition is adjusting to the different culture and environment of the business world. The military instills discipline, leadership, and a strong work ethic, which are all valuable traits for entrepreneurs. However, it is important to recognize that the business landscape operates differently from the military hierarchy. Veterans must learn to adapt their leadership style and embrace new ways of thinking to thrive in the entrepreneurial world.

Another key aspect of transitioning is identifying transferable skills from military experience to entrepreneurship. Veterans possess a wide range of skills, such as problem-solving, teamwork, and the ability to perform under pressure. These skills can be leveraged in various aspects of entrepreneurship, from project management to customer relations. Recognizing and highlighting these skills will give veterans a competitive edge in the business world.

Additionally, building a strong support network is crucial for veterans venturing into entrepreneurship. Connecting with other veteran entrepreneurs, business professionals, and mentors can provide valuable guidance, advice, and opportunities. Many organizations and networks exist specifically to support veteran entrepreneurs, offering resources, funding, and mentorship programs tailored to their unique needs. By tapping into these networks, veterans can gain access to a wealth of knowledge and support.

Finally, veterans must embrace a growth mindset and be willing to continuously learn and adapt. The entrepreneurial journey is filled with ups and downs, and it is essential to approach challenges as opportunities for growth. Seeking out learning opportunities, attending workshops, and staying updated with industry trends will help veterans stay competitive and continuously evolve their businesses.

Transitioning from the military to entrepreneurship is a rewarding and empowering path for veterans. By harnessing their unique skills, seeking support, and embracing a growth mindset, veterans can successfully navigate this transition and build thriving businesses, and achieve business success in their post-military lives.

Identifying Transferable Skills

In the journey of transitioning from military service to civilian life, one of the key challenges faced by veterans is translating their military experience into the language of the business world. While the skills acquired in the military may seem specific to the battlefield, it is essential to recognize that they possess a wide range of transferable skills that can be invaluable in the business realm. This subchapter aims to assist general readers, veterans, business people, and military personnel, particularly those who aspire to become veteran entrepreneurs, in identifying and harnessing their transferable skills for business success.

First and foremost, military service instills a sense of discipline, resilience, and adaptability. These traits are highly sought after in the business world as they enable individuals to navigate through challenges, embrace change, and persist in the face of adversity. By recognizing these qualities within themselves, veterans can position themselves as valuable assets in any entrepreneurial venture.

Leadership is another transferable skill that veterans possess in abundance. Whether they served as team leaders, squad commanders, or officers in the military, their ability to motivate, inspire, and guide others is invaluable in the business realm. The capacity to effectively communicate, delegate tasks, and make informed decisions under pressure are all qualities that make veterans natural leaders. Recognizing and leveraging these skills can significantly contribute to their success as veteran entrepreneurs.

Problem-solving and strategic thinking are also critical skills honed in the military. Veterans are trained to analyze complex situations, assess risks, and develop effective solutions. These skills are transferable to the business world, where entrepreneurs constantly face challenges and need to make strategic decisions. By capitalizing on their ability to think critically and strategically, veterans can bring a unique perspective to business and to their entrepreneurial endeavors.

Furthermore, the military fosters a strong work ethic and a commitment to teamwork. Veterans understand the importance of collaboration, cooperation, and working towards a common goal. These are highly valued skills in the business world, where teamwork and synergy drive success. By emphasizing their ability to work collaboratively, veterans can establish themselves as reliable and effective team players.

Identifying transferable skills is crucial for veterans aspiring to become successful entrepreneurs. By recognizing their discipline, resilience, adaptability, leadership, problem-solving, strategic thinking, work ethic, and teamwork, veterans can leverage their unique experiences and skills to achieve business success. The journey from military service to entrepreneurship may seem challenging, but with the right mindset and the ability to identify and harness transferable skills, veterans possess the potential to excel in the business world.

Overcoming Challenges and Adapting to Change

The ability to overcome challenges and adapt to change is crucial for success. This holds particularly true for the unique group of individuals known as veteran entrepreneurs. In the subchapter "Overcoming Challenges and Adapting to Change," we delve into the mindset and strategies necessary for these remarkable individuals to navigate the ever-evolving landscape of business.

For military personnel transitioning into the world of entrepreneurship, the journey can be both exciting and daunting. The skills gained through military service, such as discipline, resilience, and adaptability, provide a strong foundation for success. However, challenges still lie ahead. From the initial hurdles of starting a business to the ongoing obstacles faced while scaling and growing, the veteran entrepreneur must embrace change and conquer adversity with an unwavering warrior mindset.

One key aspect of overcoming challenges is embracing failure as a learning opportunity. Veterans know that setbacks are not the end but rather valuable stepping stones towards growth. In this subchapter, we explore the stories of successful veteran entrepreneurs who have turned failures into triumphs. Their experiences serve as a guiding light for those facing their own obstacles, demonstrating that resilience and determination can lead to extraordinary achievements.

In addition to embracing failure, veteran entrepreneurs must also adapt to the ever-changing business landscape. The ability to recognize trends, seize opportunities, and pivot when necessary is crucial. This subchapter offers practical advice and strategies for staying ahead of the curve. From leveraging technology to building a strong network, we explore the tools and resources available to veteran entrepreneurs to thrive in an ever-evolving business world.

Furthermore, we address the unique challenges faced by veteran entrepreneurs, such as transitioning from a structured military environment to the entrepreneurial realm, managing the emotional toll of leaving a military career behind, and balancing the demands of business ownership with personal life. By acknowledging and addressing these challenges head-on, we empower veteran entrepreneurs to navigate the path to success with confidence and clarity.

"Overcoming Challenges and Adapting to Change" is a subchapter that not only resonates with veterans but also provides valuable insights to a broader audience. Whether you are a businessperson seeking inspiration or a military personnel contemplating entrepreneurship, the lessons within this subchapter will equip you with the mindset and strategies necessary to triumph over adversity and embrace change. Through the stories of those who have walked the path before, we demonstrate that the warrior mindset is not limited to the battlefield but can also lead to remarkable business success.

Embracing the Entrepreneurial Spirit

The entrepreneurial spirit is a driving force that propels individuals to take risks, pursue their passions, and create innovative solutions to problems. In the context of veterans transitioning into the world of entrepreneurship, embracing this spirit is crucial for building successful businesses and achieving long-term business goals.

For veterans, the transition from military life to the civilian world can be challenging. However, it is important to remember that the skills and mindset acquired during military service can be invaluable assets in the business world. The discipline, adaptability, and determination instilled in veterans make them well-suited for entrepreneurial endeavors.

One of the key aspects of embracing the entrepreneurial spirit is having a clear vision. Veterans, with their strong sense of purpose and mission-driven mindset, can leverage their experiences to define their goals and objectives. By aligning their business ventures with their personal values, veterans can create a sense of meaning and purpose that drives their success.

Another crucial element is embracing risk-taking. The military often exposes veterans to high-pressure situations where quick decision-making and calculated risks are necessary for success. This ability to assess risks and make informed choices can be transferred to the business realm. By embracing calculated risks, veterans can overcome obstacles and seize opportunities that others might shy away from.

Furthermore, the entrepreneurial spirit requires a continuous pursuit of knowledge and personal growth. Veterans are accustomed to ongoing training and professional development, making them well-equipped to adapt to the ever-changing business landscape. By embracing a growth mindset, veterans can constantly learn from their experiences, seek out mentorship, and acquire new skills to stay ahead of the competition.

In addition, and I will continue to mention through the book, veterans are known for their strong work ethic and ability to work in teams. These qualities are vastly prized in the business world, where collaboration and perseverance are essential. By leveraging their teamwork skills and cultivating a network of like-minded individuals, veterans can create a supportive ecosystem that fosters growth and success.

Ultimately, embracing the entrepreneurial spirit as a veteran entrepreneur involves recognizing and capitalizing on the unique strengths and experiences gained during military service. By embracing risk, having a clear vision, continuously learning, and leveraging teamwork, veterans can navigate the challenges of entrepreneurship and build successful businesses that contribute to their personal and professional fulfillment.

Whether you are a veteran, a business person, or a military personnel interested in entrepreneurship, embracing the entrepreneurial spirit can unlock a world of opportunities. By harnessing your unique experiences and skills, you can create a business that not only achieves financial success but also embodies your values and makes a positive impact in the world.

Chapter 2: Building a Strong Foundation

Defining Your Vision and Mission

In the journey of entrepreneurship, it is crucial to have a clear vision and a well-defined mission. This subchapter will delve into the importance of defining your vision and mission, specifically tailored to the needs and experiences of the veteran entrepreneur. Whether you are a veteran transitioning into the business world or a military personnel seeking to explore entrepreneurship, this chapter will guide you towards success.

As a veteran, you possess a unique set of skills and experiences that can greatly contribute to your entrepreneurial journey. However, to effectively leverage these assets, it is essential to have a strong vision. Your vision is your ultimate goal, the destination you wish to reach. It serves as your guidepost and navigational beacon, providing you with direction and purpose. By defining your vision, you can align your actions and decisions to ensure they are in harmony with your long-term objectives.

To craft a compelling vision, start by reflecting on your passions, values, and aspirations. Consider the impact you wish to create in the world and the values you hold dear. A powerful vision should inspire and motivate you, driving you to overcome challenges and persevere in the face of adversity.

Once you have established your vision, it's time to define your mission. Your mission statement represents the path you will take to achieve your vision. It outlines the specific actions and strategies you will employ to fulfill your purpose. Your mission should be concise, yet comprehensive, encapsulating the essence of your business and the value it brings to your customers.

For the veteran entrepreneur, your mission can be shaped by your military experiences. Your leadership skills, discipline, and resilience can be integrated into your mission, setting you apart from your competitors. By leveraging these qualities, you can create a mission that resonates with your target audience and showcases your unique value proposition.

By defining your vision and mission is a crucial step towards entrepreneurial success. As a veteran entrepreneur, you have the advantage of a rich background that can be harnessed to create a powerful vision and mission statement. By aligning your actions with your long-term objectives and leveraging your military experiences, you can build a thriving business that embodies your values and contributes to your desired impact. So, take the time to reflect, define, and refine your vision and mission, and let them be the driving force behind your entrepreneurial journey.

Clarifying Your Purpose and Values

In the pursuit of success in business, it is crucial to have a clear understanding of your purpose and values. This subchapter aims to guide general readers, veterans, business people, and military personnel, especially those in the niche of the veteran entrepreneur, on how to clarify their purpose and values to achieve entrepreneurial success.

Clarifying your purpose and values is an essential step towards finding fulfillment and direction in your entrepreneurial journey. Understanding your purpose will provide you with a sense of meaning and motivation, while your values will serve as your guiding principles and moral compass.

To begin clarifying your purpose, take some time to reflect on your passions, interests, and skills. Consider the experiences and knowledge you gained during your military service and how they can be applied to your entrepreneurial endeavors. Identify what truly drives you and what impact you want to make through your business.

Next, it is important to define your values. Ask yourself what principles are most important to you and what kind of company culture you want to build. Values such as integrity, teamwork, and dedication are often instilled in military personnel and can be carried over into your entrepreneurial ventures. Clearly defining your values will not only guide your decision-making process but also help attract like-minded individuals to your business.

Additionally, understanding your purpose and values will assist you in setting meaningful goals for your business. Aligning your goals with your purpose will enhance your focus and drive, increasing the likelihood of achieving success. It will also help you make decisions that are in line with your values, ensuring that your business remains true to its core principles.

Lastly, regularly reassess your purpose and values as you progress in your entrepreneurial journey. As your business evolves, your purpose may shift, and your values may need to be reaffirmed or adjusted. By staying connected to your purpose and values, you can adapt to changes while maintaining your authenticity and integrity.

Clarifying your purpose and values is a crucial step towards achieving success as a veteran entrepreneur. By understanding what drives you and defining your guiding principles, you will be better equipped to set meaningful goals, make informed decisions, and build a business that aligns with your core values. Embrace the warrior mindset and embark on your entrepreneurial journey with a clear sense of purpose and unwavering values.

Setting Long-Term Goals and Objectives

In the journey towards entrepreneurship, setting long-term goals and objectives is a crucial step that can pave the way for success. Whether you are a veteran transitioning into civilian life or a business person looking to enter the realm of entrepreneurship, having a clear vision and a roadmap for the future is paramount. This subchapter will delve into the importance of setting long-term goals and objectives and provide valuable insights for the veteran entrepreneur.

For veterans, the military background instills a unique set of skills and qualities that can be invaluable in the business world. However, transitioning from military service to entrepreneurship requires careful planning and a solid understanding of long-term goals. Setting objectives that align with your passion, values, and skill set is essential for creating a successful business venture. This subchapter will guide veterans through the process of identifying their strengths, exploring their interests, and defining their long-term goals, ensuring a smooth transition into the world of entrepreneurship.

Business people, too, can benefit greatly from setting long-term goals and objectives. Whether you are an established professional or someone seeking a career change, having a clear vision for your future can provide focus and direction. This subchapter will explore proven strategies for setting ambitious yet achievable long-term goals, along with practical tips to stay motivated and overcome obstacles along the way.

Moreover, military personnel currently serving can also greatly benefit from understanding the importance of setting long-term goals and objectives. While their immediate focus may be on their military duties, having a vision beyond their service can provide a sense of purpose and direction, ensuring a seamless transition into entrepreneurship or other career paths after military service.

"The Veteran Entrepreneur" niche is a unique blend of military experience and entrepreneurial aspirations. This subchapter will address the specific challenges and opportunities that veteran entrepreneurs may encounter. It will discuss the importance of leveraging military skills, such as discipline, leadership, and adaptability, while setting long-term goals and objectives for their business ventures.

setting long-term goals and objectives is a vital step towards achieving success in entrepreneurship. Whether you are a veteran, business person, or military personnel, understanding the significance of long-term planning and having a clear vision for the future is paramount. This subchapter will equip you with the necessary tools, strategies, and inspiration to set meaningful long-term goals and objectives, ensuring a fulfilling and prosperous entrepreneurial journey.

Creating a Compelling Mission Statement

Having a clear and compelling mission statement is crucial for success. A mission statement serves as the foundation of any business, providing direction, purpose, and a sense of identity. For the veteran entrepreneur, crafting such a statement is even more critical, as it can draw upon the unique qualities and experiences gained during military service.

A compelling mission statement encapsulates the essence of your business, reflecting its values, goals, and aspirations. It should be concise, yet powerful enough to inspire and engage both your team and your target audience. As a veteran entrepreneur, your mission statement can leverage the strengths and skills cultivated during your military career, setting you apart from the competition.

One key aspect to consider when creating a mission statement is to reflect on the values and principles that guided you during your military service. Honor, integrity, discipline, and teamwork are just a few examples of the values that can be incorporated into your mission statement. By doing so, you not only honor your military background but also establish a strong foundation for your business.

Additionally, a compelling mission statement should clearly define the purpose and goals of your business. What problem are you solving? What unique value do you bring to the market? How do you plan to make a difference? These are questions that your mission statement should address, allowing your audience to understand your business's purpose and its relevance in the market.

Furthermore, a mission statement should be authentic and genuine. It should reflect your passion, beliefs, and vision for the future. As a veteran entrepreneur, you possess a unique perspective and determination that can be conveyed through your mission statement. This authenticity will resonate with your audience, building trust and loyalty.

Ultimately, a compelling mission statement for the veteran entrepreneur should be a reflection of your military background, values, and business goals. By leveraging the strengths gained during your service, you can create a mission statement that sets you apart from the competition while inspiring and engaging those around you.

Developing a Strategic Business Plan

In the competitive world of entrepreneurship, it is crucial to have a well-defined strategic business plan. This subchapter aims to guide general individuals, veterans, business people, and military personnel, especially those who identify themselves as veteran entrepreneurs, in developing an effective strategic business plan that sets them on the path to success.

A strategic business plan acts as a roadmap for your business, outlining your goals, objectives, and the strategies you will employ to achieve them. It provides a clear direction and helps you make informed decisions, allocate resources effectively, and navigate the challenges that arise along the way.

The first step in developing a strategic business plan is to identify your mission and vision. Define the purpose of your business and the values that drive you. This will serve as a guiding light, keeping you focused and motivated throughout your entrepreneurial journey.

Next, conduct a thorough analysis of your target market, competition, and industry trends. Understand the needs and desires of your customers, and identify any gaps in the market that your business can fill. This analysis will help you position your business strategically and differentiate yourself from competitors.

Once you have a clear understanding of your market, it's time to set specific, measurable, achievable, relevant, and time-bound (SMART) goals. These goals should align with your mission and vision and provide a clear direction for your business. Break down your long-term goals into short-term objectives, making them more manageable and easier to track.

After setting your goals, develop strategies and action plans to achieve them. Consider your marketing, sales, operations, and financial strategies, among others. Ensure that these strategies are aligned with your goals and leverage your strengths to gain a competitive advantage.

Regularly review and revise your strategic business plan as your business evolves and the market changes. Continuously monitor your progress, measure your key performance indicators, and adjust your strategies accordingly. A strategic business plan is not static; it should be adaptable and flexible to ensure your business's long-term success.

Therefore, developing a strategic business plan is a fundamental step for any entrepreneur, particularly for veteran entrepreneurs. It provides a roadmap for success, guiding your business towards your goals and objectives. By understanding your market, setting SMART goals, and implementing well-defined strategies, you can position yourself as a formidable player in your industry. Regularly reviewing and revising your plan will help you stay ahead of the competition and navigate the ever-changing business landscape.

Conducting Market Research and Analysis

Market research and analysis play a vital role in the success of any business, including those founded by veteran entrepreneurs. By thoroughly understanding the market, its trends, and the needs of potential customers, veterans can make informed decisions and create strategies that set them up for success.

Understanding the market starts with identifying the target audience. Whether you're offering a product or service, understanding who your customers are and what they want is essential. As a veteran entrepreneur, you possess a unique perspective and insight that can be leveraged to identify niches within the market that may have been overlooked. By focusing on these niches, you can tailor your offerings to meet the specific needs of your target audience, setting your business apart from the competition.

Once you have identified your target audience, conducting market research will help you gain a deeper understanding of their behavior, preferences, and purchasing habits. Various methods can be employed, such as surveys, interviews, and focus groups, to collect valuable data. Additionally, analyzing data from industry reports, competitor analysis, and online research can provide valuable insights into market trends, pricing strategies, and potential opportunities.

Market analysis is not a one-time process but an ongoing effort. As a veteran entrepreneur, you need to stay updated with the ever-changing market dynamics. By continuously monitoring changes in customer preferences, emerging trends, and new technologies, you can adapt your business strategies and stay ahead of the competition.

Furthermore, market research and analysis can help you identify potential risks and challenges that your business may face. By understanding the market landscape, you can proactively develop contingency plans to mitigate risks and ensure your business remains resilient.

For veterans transitioning into entrepreneurship, market research and analysis can be a valuable tool to bridge the gap between military experience and business success. The discipline, attention to detail, and analytical skills honed during military service can be applied to conducting thorough market research and analysis, giving veterans a competitive edge in the business world.

By understanding the target audience, identifying niches, and staying updated with market trends, veterans can make informed decisions and develop strategies that lead to long-term business success. Embracing the warrior mindset, veterans can leverage their unique perspectives and experiences to navigate the complexities of entrepreneurship and achieve their business goals.

Identifying Target Customers and Niche Markets

Understanding your target customers and finding your niche market is of utmost importance for the success of any venture. This subchapter will guide you through the process of identifying your target customers and niche markets, with a special focus on the unique perspective and opportunities available to veteran entrepreneurs.

As a veteran entrepreneur, you already possess a distinct advantage - your military background! This experience has equipped you with valuable skills, discipline, and a strong work ethic that can set you apart in the business world. By leveraging your military expertise, you can identify target customers who can benefit from your specialized knowledge and skills.

To start, take a closer look at your own experiences and interests. Reflect on the specific challenges you faced during your military service and the solutions you developed. Consider how these experiences can be translated into products or services that cater to the needs of a specific target audience. For instance, if you were part of a logistics team, you could explore opportunities in supply chain management or transportation services. If you were are intelligence analyst, your skill could very easily lend themselves to business intelligence and other disciplines.

Next, conduct thorough market research to identify potential niche markets that align with your skills and experiences. Look for gaps or underserved areas within industries where your expertise can be applied. For example, if you have a background in cybersecurity, you might consider targeting small businesses that lack the resources to hire a full-time IT team.

Additionally, networking with fellow veterans and industry professionals can provide valuable insights and connections. Attend industry events, join veteran entrepreneurship organizations, and engage with online communities to gain a deeper understanding of the market and identify potential customers.

Once you have identified your target customers and niche markets, it is essential to tailor your marketing strategies accordingly. Craft a compelling message that highlights the unique value you bring as a veteran entrepreneur. Emphasize how your military background translates into credibility, reliability, and a commitment to excellence.

Remember, the key to success lies in focusing on a specific niche rather than trying to appeal to a broad audience. By targeting a specific customer segment with tailored solutions, you can establish yourself as an expert in that area, building trust and loyalty among your customers.

Identifying target customers and niche markets is crucial for the success of any business, especially for veteran entrepreneurs. Leverage your military experience, conduct thorough market research, and tailor your strategies to effectively serve your target audience. By doing so, you can capitalize on your unique strengths and experiences, setting yourself up for business success.

Crafting a Competitive Strategy

Having a well-crafted and effective competitive strategy is crucial for success. In this subchapter, we will explore the importance of developing a competitive strategy and how it can benefit the veteran entrepreneur.

As a veteran, you possess a unique set of skills and experiences that can give you a competitive edge in the business world. However, it is essential to understand that being a veteran alone is not enough to guarantee success. Crafting a competitive strategy will enable you to leverage your strengths and overcome any obstacles that may come your way.

One of the first steps in developing a competitive strategy is to conduct a thorough analysis of the market landscape. This involves identifying your target audience, understanding their needs and preferences, and evaluating the strengths and weaknesses of your competitors. By gaining a deep understanding of the market, you can identify opportunities and position yourself in a way that differentiates you from others.

Another important aspect of crafting a competitive strategy is defining your unique selling proposition (USP). Your USP is what sets you apart from your competitors and gives customers a compelling reason to choose your products or services. As a veteran entrepreneur, you can leverage your military experience to create a USP that resonates with your target audience, such as emphasizing qualities like discipline, leadership, and problem-solving skills.

Additionally, crafting a competitive strategy involves setting clear goals and objectives for your business. These goals should be specific, measurable, attainable, relevant, and time-bound (SMART). By setting SMART goals, you can track your progress and make necessary adjustments to stay on track.

Furthermore, it is crucial to continually monitor and evaluate your competitive strategy. The business landscape is constantly evolving, and what may have worked initially may not be effective in the long run. Regularly reassessing your strategy will help you adapt to changes in the market and stay ahead of the competition.

Crafting a competitive strategy is essential for the veteran entrepreneur looking to succeed in the business world. By conducting a thorough market analysis, defining a unique selling proposition, setting SMART goals, and regularly evaluating your strategy, you can position yourself for long-term success. Remember, being a veteran gives you a solid foundation, but a well-crafted competitive strategy will help you thrive in the entrepreneurial battlefield.

Chapter 3: The Art of Leadership

Leading by Example

The ability to lead by example is a crucial skill that can make or break the success of a business. This subchapter explores the importance of leading by example and how it can be harnessed to achieve business success. Drawing upon the experiences of veterans who have transitioned into the world of entrepreneurship, we delve into the unique insights and strategies they have developed to thrive in this competitive landscape.

For veterans turned entrepreneurs, leading by example is ingrained in their DNA. Having served in the military, they have witnessed firsthand the transformative power of strong leadership, as well as the destructive power of bad leadership. In the face of adversity, veterans have learned to lead from the front, demonstrating unwavering commitment, discipline, and resilience. These qualities are equally applicable in the realm of business, where leading by example can inspire and motivate teams to achieve extraordinary results.

One of the key lessons from veterans who have successfully transitioned into entrepreneurship is the importance of aligning actions with words. It is not enough to simply give orders or outline a vision; true leaders must embody the values they espouse. By leading by example, veterans-turned-entrepreneurs have fostered a culture of trust and respect within their organizations, empowering their teams to be the best versions of themselves.

Leading by example also involves taking calculated risks, an attribute veterans are well-acquainted with. In their military service, they have been trained to make critical decisions under pressure. This experience translates seamlessly into the world of business, where calculated risks are often necessary for growth and innovation. By fearlessly stepping into uncharted territory, veteran entrepreneurs inspire their teams to embrace risk-taking and push the boundaries of what is possible.

Moreover, leading by example extends beyond the confines of the workplace. Veterans who have embraced entrepreneurship understand the importance of giving back to their communities. By engaging in philanthropic endeavors, they inspire others to follow suit and create a positive impact in the world. This chapter explores various ways in which veteran entrepreneurs have leveraged their leadership skills to make a difference in society.

Leading by example is an invaluable trait that sets veteran entrepreneurs apart from the rest. Drawing upon their military experience, they inspire and motivate others to achieve greatness. By aligning actions with words, taking calculated risks, and giving back, veteran entrepreneurs exemplify the qualities required for business success. Whether you are a veteran, a business person, a military personnel, or simply seeking inspiration, this chapter provides profound insights into the power of leading by example and its transformative effects on entrepreneurship.

Demonstrating Integrity and Ethical Behavior

Integrity and ethical behavior are crucial for long-term success. This is especially true for veterans transitioning into entrepreneurship. As a veteran entrepreneur, your background instills a strong sense of discipline, honor, and a commitment to doing what is right. By harnessing these values, you can build a solid foundation for your business and gain the trust and respect of your customers and stakeholders.

Integrity is the cornerstone of any successful business. It means being honest, transparent, and acting with moral principles at all times. As a veteran, you have already proven your dedication to upholding these values in the military. Now, it's time to apply them to your business ventures.

Maintaining integrity in business is not always easy, especially when faced with tough decisions or temptations. However, it is during these moments that your character shines through. By making ethical choices, even if they are difficult or unpopular, you demonstrate your commitment to doing what is right, which ultimately builds trust and credibility in your brand.

One way to demonstrate integrity is through transparent and honest communication. Be open and upfront with your customers, employees, and stakeholders. Share your values, mission, and goals with them, and always deliver on your promises. Building a reputation for integrity and ethical behavior will not only attract loyal customers but also inspire loyalty and dedication from your team.

Ethical behavior goes beyond honesty and transparency. It means treating all individuals, whether they are customers, employees, or suppliers, with respect and fairness. As a veteran entrepreneur, you understand the importance of teamwork and collaboration. By fostering a culture of inclusivity, equality, and fairness within your organization, you create an environment where everyone feels valued and motivated to contribute their best.

Furthermore, ethical behavior extends to your business practices. Ensure that your operations comply with legal and ethical standards. Avoid cutting corners or engaging in fraudulent activities. Your commitment to ethical practices will not only protect your business from legal repercussions but also build a reputation for trustworthiness and reliability.

As a veteran entrepreneur, demonstrating integrity and ethical behavior is crucial for long-term success. By upholding these values, you build trust and credibility in your brand, attract loyal customers, and inspire dedication from your team. Remember, integrity is not just about doing what is right when it is convenient – it is about consistently making ethical choices, even when faced with challenges. By embodying these principles, you can create a business that not only thrives financially but also makes a positive impact on the world.

Inspiring and Motivating Others

In the pursuit of entrepreneurial success, one of the most valuable skills you can possess is the ability to inspire and motivate others. Whether you are a veteran, a businessperson, or a military personnel transitioning into entrepreneurship, understanding how to ignite the fire within individuals and teams is crucial for achieving your goals. This subchapter explores key strategies and techniques to inspire and motivate others, ultimately fostering a positive and driven environment that propels your business towards success.

As a veteran entrepreneur, you possess a unique set of qualities that can inspire and motivate those around you. Your experiences in the military have shaped you into a resilient, disciplined, and determined individual. Sharing your story, highlighting the challenges you've overcome, and emphasizing the lessons you've learned can serve as a powerful source of inspiration for others. By demonstrating your ability to triumph over adversity, you instill a sense of belief and motivation in those who look up to you.

Another effective way to inspire and motivate others is by setting a compelling vision for your business. Clearly communicate your goals, values, and mission to your team, customers, and stakeholders. Paint a picture of the future you are striving to create and explain how their participation is vital to achieving that vision. When people understand the purpose behind their work and how it contributes to a greater cause, they are more likely to stay motivated and give their best effort.

Furthermore, recognizing and celebrating the achievements and contributions of your team members is essential to maintaining a motivated workforce. Regularly acknowledge and reward their efforts, whether through verbal praise, incentives, or growth opportunities. By fostering a culture of appreciation and recognition, you create an environment where individuals feel valued and motivated to continue pushing themselves.

In addition to personal recognition, providing opportunities for growth and development is crucial for inspiring and motivating others. Encourage your team members to expand their skills, pursue new challenges, and take on responsibilities that align with their interests and aspirations. By investing in their professional growth, you not only enhance their motivation but also foster a sense of loyalty and commitment to your business.

Lastly, lead by example. Your actions, work ethic, and dedication should serve as a constant source of inspiration for others. Show them what it means to be a warrior in the business world – resilient, adaptable, and relentless in the pursuit of success. Your passion and determination will undoubtedly inspire those around you and motivate them to push beyond their limits.

Inspiring and motivating others is a vital skill for any veteran entrepreneur. By sharing your story, setting a compelling vision, recognizing achievements, providing growth opportunities, and leading by example, you can create a positive and driven environment that propels your business towards success. Remember, as a veteran, you possess a unique set of qualities that can inspire and motivate others – embrace them and inspire others to do the same.

Effective Communication and Active Listening

Effective communication is an essential skill for success. Whether you are a veteran entrepreneur, a business professional, or a military personnel, mastering the art of communication will significantly enhance your chances of achieving your goals and building strong relationships.

Communication is not just about speaking; it also involves active listening. Active listening is the ability to fully concentrate, understand, and respond to what others are saying. This skill forms the foundation of effective communication and is crucial for building trust and fostering collaboration.

One of the key aspects of effective communication is clarity. When conveying your thoughts, ideas, or instructions, it is essential to be concise and articulate. Avoid using jargon or technical terms that may confuse your audience. Instead, use simple language and provide clear examples to ensure your message is easily understood by everyone.

Active listening goes hand in hand with effective communication. It involves giving your undivided attention to the person speaking, showing genuine interest, and avoiding distractions. By listening actively, you not only understand the content of the message but also the emotions and intentions behind it. This understanding allows you to respond appropriately and build meaningful connections with others.

As a veteran entrepreneur, your military experience has likely honed your communication skills. The ability to communicate effectively under pressure and in high-stake situations is a valuable asset in the business world. However, it is essential to adapt your communication style to the civilian environment. Be mindful of cultural differences, avoid military jargon, and be open to different perspectives.

In the realm of entrepreneurship, effective communication and active listening play a critical role in various aspects of your business. Whether it's negotiating deals, resolving conflicts, or managing a team, your ability to communicate clearly and listen actively will determine your success.

To enhance your communication skills, consider seeking feedback from trusted mentors or colleagues. Actively ask for their input on your communication style and make adjustments accordingly. Additionally, invest time in reading books, attending workshops, or enrolling in courses that focus on communication and active listening.

Remember, effective communication and active listening are lifelong skills that require constant practice and refinement. By mastering these skills, you will not only become a more successful entrepreneur but also build strong and lasting connections with others.

Building and Managing High-Performing Teams

The ability to build and manage high-performing teams is a crucial skill for any entrepreneur, especially for those with a military background. In this subchapter, we will explore the importance of teamwork, strategies for building effective teams, and techniques for managing and inspiring team members to achieve exceptional results.

As veterans, we understand the value of teamwork and the power of collaboration. We have experienced firsthand how a cohesive unit can accomplish missions that seem impossible. Translating this mindset into the business world is essential for veteran entrepreneurs looking to achieve success.

Building a high-performing team starts with selecting the right individuals. Look for team members who possess the necessary skills, experience, and values that align with your business objectives.

Veterans, in particular, bring unique qualities such as discipline, adaptability, and resilience, which can greatly contribute to the success of a team.

Once the team is assembled, it is essential to foster an environment that encourages open communication, trust, and mutual respect. Encourage team members to share their ideas and perspectives, creating a culture of innovation and collaboration. Regular team meetings and brainstorming sessions can serve as platforms for idea exchange and problem-solving.

Furthermore, effective team management involves setting clear expectations and goals. Clearly define roles and responsibilities, ensuring that each team member understands their contribution to the overall mission. Regularly assess individual and team performance, providing constructive feedback and recognition for achievements.

To maximize team performance, it is crucial to nurture a sense of camaraderie and support among team members. Encourage collaboration and cooperation, fostering an environment where individuals feel comfortable seeking help and sharing knowledge. By promoting a culture of continuous learning and growth, you can create a team that is motivated to excel and surpass their own expectations.

Effective team management also includes recognizing and leveraging the strengths of each team member. Assign tasks and projects that align with their skills and expertise, allowing them to thrive in their designated roles. By empowering and inspiring team members to utilize their strengths, you can unlock their full potential and drive exceptional results.

Building and managing high-performing teams is an essential aspect of business success for veteran entrepreneurs. By applying the principles of teamwork, effective communication, and trust, along with leveraging the unique strengths of each team member, you can create a cohesive unit that is capable of achieving remarkable goals. Embrace the warrior mindset, and let it guide you in building and managing a team that will propel your entrepreneurial journey towards unprecedented success.

Recruiting and Selecting the Right Team Members

Building a successful business requires a solid foundation, and that starts with assembling the right team. Whether you're a general audience member, a veteran, a business person, or military personnel, finding the perfect team members is crucial for your success as a veteran entrepreneur. This subchapter will guide you through the process of recruiting and selecting the right individuals who will complement your skills and contribute to your business growth.

The first step in recruiting the right team members is to define the roles and responsibilities within your organization. As a veteran entrepreneur, you understand the importance of clear objectives and a strategic approach. Identify the specific skill sets and expertise needed to achieve your business goals, and create job descriptions that reflect those requirements.

When it comes to selecting team members, consider the values and principles that align with your business mission. As a veteran, you possess a unique perspective on discipline, integrity, and teamwork. Seek individuals who share those values and can contribute to a positive and productive work environment.

Networking is a powerful tool for finding potential team members. Leverage your military connections, attend industry events, and join relevant organizations to expand your network. Engage in conversations, listen to others' experiences, and identify individuals who demonstrate a strong work ethic and a passion for entrepreneurship.

Once you have identified potential candidates, conduct thorough interviews to assess their qualifications and cultural fit. Ask open-ended questions that allow them to showcase their skills, problem-solving abilities, and their ability to adapt to a dynamic business environment. Additionally, consider conducting background checks and contacting references to ensure their credibility and reliability.

As a veteran entrepreneur, building a diverse team is essential for fostering innovation and creativity. Diversity contributes to a broad range of perspectives and experiences, which can lead to more effective problem-solving and decision-making. Embrace diversity in your team and create an inclusive work environment that values different ideas and backgrounds.

Finally, remember that building a successful team is an ongoing process. Continuously evaluate your team members' performance, provide constructive feedback, and offer opportunities for growth and development. Encourage open communication and collaboration to foster a sense of camaraderie and shared purpose.

Recruiting and selecting the right team members is a critical aspect of entrepreneurial success for veterans. By defining roles, seeking individuals who share your values, leveraging your network, conducting thorough interviews, embracing diversity, and nurturing your team's growth, you will be on the path to building a strong and cohesive team that drives your business towards success.

Fostering Collaboration and Trust

Collaboration and trust are essential ingredients for success. Whether you are a veteran entrepreneur, a business person, or a military personnel transitioning into the civilian workforce, understanding how to foster collaboration and trust within your team or organization is crucial.

Collaboration is the act of working together towards a common goal. It involves leveraging the diverse skills, experiences, and perspectives of individuals to achieve a collective outcome. As a veteran entrepreneur, you already possess valuable qualities such as discipline, leadership, and teamwork, which can greatly contribute to fostering collaboration.

To foster collaboration, it is important to create an environment that encourages open communication and mutual respect. This means promoting a culture where everyone's ideas and opinions are valued, regardless of rank or position. Encourage your team members to actively participate in discussions, brainstorming sessions, and decision-making processes. By doing so, you not only tap into the collective wisdom of your team but also empower them to take ownership of their work.

Trust is the foundation upon which successful collaborations are built. As a veteran, you understand the importance of trust, especially in high-stakes situations. To foster trust within your team, lead by example. Be transparent, honest, and reliable in your actions and communication. Demonstrate your commitment to the team's success and show that you value and support each team member.

Another way to build trust is through effective delegation. Delegate tasks and responsibilities based on individual strengths and skills, allowing team members to showcase their expertise and contribute to the overall success. This not only fosters a sense of ownership and empowerment but also builds trust as team members feel valued and respected.

Building collaboration and trust also involves fostering a sense of camaraderie and shared purpose. Encourage team-building activities, such as social events, workshops, or volunteer initiatives. These activities can help forge stronger relationships among team members and create a supportive and cohesive work environment.

Fostering collaboration and trust is vital for any veteran entrepreneur or business person. By creating an environment that encourages open communication, mutual respect, and trust, you can harness the power of collaboration to drive success in your business endeavors. Remember, collaboration is not just about working together; it is about leveraging the diverse strengths and skills of your team to achieve greater outcomes. With trust as the foundation, you can build a strong and cohesive team that is capable of overcoming any challenge and achieving long-term success in the business world.

Resolving Conflicts and Promoting Unity

In business conflicts are bound to arise. Whether it's a disagreement with a business partner, a clash with a client, or a difference of opinion within your team, conflicts can impact the success of your venture. As a veteran entrepreneur, you possess a unique set of skills and experiences that can be leveraged to effectively resolve conflicts and promote unity within your business.

One of the key lessons you learned during your military service is the importance of clear communication. Apply this principle to your entrepreneurial endeavors by fostering an environment where open and honest dialogue is encouraged. Encourage your team members to express their concerns, ideas, and perspectives, and actively listen to their input. By doing so, you create a platform for understanding and collaboration, mitigating potential conflicts before they escalate.

Additionally, as a veteran, you understand the value of teamwork and the power of diverse perspectives. Embrace the diversity within your team and leverage it as a strength. Encourage your employees to contribute their unique skills and experiences, creating a culture that values and respects different viewpoints. By promoting unity and inclusivity, you foster an environment where conflicts are less likely to arise and where creativity and innovation can thrive.

When conflicts do arise, it's crucial to address them head-on and in a timely manner. Avoiding or ignoring conflicts can lead to resentment and further escalation. Instead, approach conflicts with a solution-oriented mindset. Encourage all parties involved to voice their concerns and work together to find a mutually beneficial resolution. By focusing on finding common ground and compromising when necessary, you can transform conflicts into opportunities for growth and improvement.

In the military, you learned the importance of discipline and self-control. Apply these principles to conflict resolution by remaining calm and composed in challenging situations. By keeping your emotions in check and approaching conflicts with a level-headed mindset, you can navigate difficult conversations and reach resolutions that are fair and beneficial for all parties involved.

Resolving conflicts and promoting unity is essential for the success of any business, and as a veteran entrepreneur, you possess the skills and mindset to excel in this area. By fostering open communication, embracing diversity, addressing conflicts directly, and approaching them with discipline and self-control, you can create a harmonious work environment that drives your business towards success.

Chapter 4: Financial Management and Planning

Understanding Business Finances

Understanding and effectively managing your business finances is crucial to achieving long-term success. This subchapter aims to provide you with a comprehensive guide to understanding business finances, tailored specifically for veterans transitioning into entrepreneurship. Whether you are a veteran, businessperson, military personnel, or simply someone interested in the veteran entrepreneur niche, this subchapter will equip you with the knowledge and tools necessary to navigate the financial aspects of your business.

The first key concept to grasp is financial literacy. This refers to the ability to understand and interpret financial statements, such as income statements, balance sheets, and cash flow statements. By developing financial literacy, you will be able to make informed decisions regarding your business's financial health and growth potential.

Next, we delve into the importance of budgeting and forecasting. Establishing a realistic budget allows you to allocate resources effectively and plan for future expenses. By forecasting your business's financial performance, you can anticipate potential challenges and opportunities, enabling you to make proactive decisions to ensure the sustainability of your venture.

Another critical aspect of understanding business finances is managing cash flow. Cash flow management involves monitoring the inflow and outflow of funds in your business. By maintaining a positive cash flow, you can ensure that you have enough working capital to cover expenses

"]

and invest in growth opportunities. This subchapter will provide you with practical tips and techniques for effective cash flow management.

Furthermore, we explore different funding options available to veteran entrepreneurs. From small business loans to crowdfunding and government grants, understanding the various funding sources and eligibility criteria will empower you to secure the necessary capital to start or expand your business.

Finally, this subchapter addresses the importance of financial controls and accountability. Implementing internal controls and regularly reviewing financial processes and reports will help you identify and mitigate any financial risks. Additionally, we discuss the significance of hiring financial professionals, such as accountants or bookkeepers, to ensure accurate financial record keeping and compliance with relevant regulations.

By the end of this subchapter, you will have a solid foundation in understanding business finances, enabling you to make informed decisions that will drive the success and growth of your veteran-owned business. Whether you are starting a new venture or looking to enhance your existing business's financial management, this subchapter will equip you with the tools and knowledge needed to navigate the complex world of business finances with confidence.

Creating a Budget and Tracking Expenses

One of the fundamental aspects of running a successful business is the ability to effectively manage finances. This holds true for everyone, whether you are a general business person, a military personnel, or a veteran looking to venture into entrepreneurship. Understanding the importance of creating a budget and tracking expenses is crucial in ensuring the long-term success and sustainability of your business.

Budgeting is essentially a roadmap that allows you to plan and allocate your financial resources in a way that aligns with your business goals. By creating a budget, you gain a clear understanding of your income and expenses, enabling you to make informed decisions about where to allocate your funds. This process helps you identify areas of potential overspending or areas where you can cut costs to maximize profitability.

For veterans transitioning into entrepreneurship, the budgeting process can be particularly beneficial. Many veterans possess a unique set of skills and experiences acquired during their military service, but transitioning into the business world can present its own set of challenges. Creating a budget provides a structure and framework to help veterans navigate this new terrain and make sound financial decisions.

Tracking expenses is another vital aspect of financial management. It involves consistently monitoring and recording all business-related expenditures. Tracking expenses allows you to identify patterns, trends, and areas where you may be overspending. Armed with this knowledge, you can take proactive measures to control costs, negotiate better deals with suppliers, or explore alternative options to optimize your budget.

The book "Warrior Mindset, Business Success: A Veteran's Guide to Entrepreneurship" recognizes the unique perspective and skills that veterans bring to the table. It emphasizes the importance of creating a budget and tracking expenses as part of a holistic approach to business success. By providing practical tips, strategies, and real-life examples, the book equips veterans with the tools they need to effectively manage their finances and build a thriving business.

Whether you are a general business person, a military personnel, or a veteran, mastering the art of budgeting and expense tracking is crucial for long-term success. By implementing these practices, you gain better control over your finances, make informed decisions, and ultimately, pave the way for a prosperous entrepreneurial journey.

Managing Cash Flow and Profitability

Cash flow and profitability are crucial aspects of running a successful business. In this subchapter, we will explore the key strategies and techniques for managing cash flow and ensuring profitability, specifically tailored to the unique needs and challenges faced by veteran entrepreneurs.

As a veteran entrepreneur, you possess a distinct set of skills and experiences that can greatly contribute to your business's success. However, understanding and effectively managing your cash flow and profitability is essential to sustaining and growing your venture.

One of the first steps in managing cash flow is to create a comprehensive budget. This budget should outline your projected income and expenses, enabling you to identify potential cash flow gaps and plan accordingly. By closely monitoring your budget, you can make informed decisions on expenditures, reduce unnecessary costs, and ensure that you have enough cash on hand to cover your expenses.

Implementing efficient cash flow management practices is crucial for long-term success. This includes invoicing promptly and following up on overdue payments, negotiating favorable payment terms with suppliers, and monitoring inventory levels to avoid tying up excess cash in unsold products. Additionally, establishing strong relationships with financial institutions and exploring financing options can provide access to capital during times of need.

Profitability is the lifeblood of any business, and it is essential to analyze and optimize your profit margins. By regularly reviewing your pricing strategy, cost structure, and identifying areas for cost reduction, you can improve your bottom line. Implementing effective marketing and sales strategies can also boost profitability by attracting new customers and increasing sales.

Furthermore, it is crucial to develop a resilient mindset when managing cash flow and profitability. As a veteran, you have already demonstrated your ability to adapt and overcome challenges. Apply this mindset to your business, staying agile and proactive in identifying potential issues before they become major problems.

Managing cash flow and profitability is a critical aspect of running a successful business, particularly for veteran entrepreneurs. By implementing sound financial practices, closely monitoring your budget, and keeping a resilient mindset, you can ensure the long-term sustainability and growth of your venture. Remember, your unique experiences and skills as a veteran entrepreneur position you for success – and with a solid grasp of cash flow and profitability management, you can truly excel in the world of entrepreneurship.

Utilizing Financial Tools and Technologies

Staying ahead of the competition requires not only determination and resilience but also the ability to leverage the latest financial tools and technologies. As a veteran entrepreneur, you possess a unique set of skills and experiences that can be harnessed to make informed financial decisions and drive your business towards success.

This subchapter explores the various financial tools and technologies available to veteran entrepreneurs, offering guidance on how to effectively utilize them to streamline operations, optimize financial management, and enhance overall business performance.

One of the key financial tools that every entrepreneur should be familiar with is accounting software. These advanced software packages enable you to track income and expenses, generate financial reports, and manage cash flow more efficiently. By utilizing accounting software, you can gain real-time insights into your business's financial health, enabling you to make data-driven decisions and identify areas for improvement.

Another essential financial tool is online banking and payment platforms. With the rise of e-commerce and digital transactions, it is crucial for veteran entrepreneurs to embrace these technologies. Online banking platforms provide convenience, allowing you to access your business accounts and conduct transactions anywhere, anytime. Payment platforms such as PayPal and Stripe enable you to accept online payments securely, expanding your customer base and boosting revenue.

Furthermore, leveraging financial technologies like cloud-based storage and data analytics can significantly enhance your business operations. Cloud storage allows you to store and access financial documents securely, eliminating the need for physical paperwork and reducing the risk of data loss. Data analytics tools enable you to analyze financial data, identify trends, and make informed predictions, empowering you to make strategic business decisions.

Additionally, exploring funding options tailored for veteran entrepreneurs can help you secure the necessary capital to grow your business. From government-backed loans to veteran-specific grants and crowdfunding platforms, there are various avenues to explore. Understanding the eligibility requirements and benefits of each option can greatly increase your chances of obtaining funding.

By utilizing these financial tools and technologies, veteran entrepreneurs can gain a competitive edge and propel their businesses towards success. Embracing digital solutions not only streamlines financial processes but also enables you to make data-driven decisions, optimize cash flow, and allocate resources more efficiently. In the dynamic world of entrepreneurship, staying ahead of the curve with financial tools and technologies is essential for sustained growth and profitability.

Securing Funding and Investment

For many veteran entrepreneurs, the path to business success starts with securing funding and investment. Whether you are starting a small business or launching a new venture, having access to capital is crucial to turning your ideas into reality. In this subchapter, we will explore various strategies and resources available to help veterans secure the funding they need to fuel their entrepreneurial journey.

As a veteran, you possess unique qualities that make you an attractive candidate for funding and investment opportunities. Your military background has equipped you with valuable skills such as discipline, leadership, and adaptability, which can greatly enhance your chances of securing financial support. However, it is important to understand the different options available and how to leverage them effectively.

One of the first steps in securing funding is to develop a comprehensive business plan. This document will serve as a roadmap for your business and demonstrate to potential investors or lenders that you have a clear vision and strategy. It should include details about your target market, competitive analysis, financial projections, and how you plan to utilize the funds. A well-crafted business plan can significantly increase your credibility and attractiveness to investors.

In addition to traditional funding sources like banks and lending institutions, veterans have access to unique resources tailored specifically to their needs. The Small Business Administration (SBA) provides various loan programs and initiatives, including the Patriot Express Loan Program, which offers favorable terms and conditions for veterans. Additionally, there are numerous grants and funding opportunities available exclusively for veteran entrepreneurs.

Networking and building relationships within the business community can also be instrumental in securing funding. Attend industry events, join veteran entrepreneur organizations, and connect with mentors who can offer guidance and potential investment opportunities. Building a strong network can open doors and provide valuable connections to individuals who share your passion for entrepreneurship.

Lastly, consider alternative funding options such as crowdfunding and angel investors. Crowdfunding platforms allow you to raise capital by appealing to a broad audience of potential investors who believe in your business idea. Angel investors, on the other hand, are individuals or groups who provide capital in exchange for equity or ownership in your company. These alternative funding methods can be particularly useful if you have a unique or innovative business concept.

Securing funding and investment is a critical step in the journey of a veteran entrepreneur. By leveraging your military background, developing a comprehensive business plan, exploring unique resources, networking, and considering alternative funding options, you can increase your chances of turning your entrepreneurial dreams into reality. Remember, perseverance and a warrior mindset are key to overcoming challenges and achieving business success.

Exploring Financing Options

In the journey of entrepreneurship, one of the key challenges faced by veteran entrepreneurs is securing adequate financing to turn their business dreams into reality. Whether you are a general audience, a veteran, a business person, or military personnel, understanding the various financing options available to you is crucial in setting the foundation for your business success. This subchapter aims to guide you through the maze of financing options, helping you make informed decisions and choose the best path forward.

1. Traditional Bank Loans: This is the most common avenue for securing financing, especially for veterans with a solid credit history. However, the application process can be lengthy and requires extensive documentation. Veterans can leverage their military service to access special loan programs specifically designed for them, such as the Small Business Administration (SBA) Veterans Advantage Loan Program.

2. Crowdfunding: With the rise of online platforms like Kickstarter and Indiegogo, crowdfunding has become a popular way to raise capital. By presenting your business idea to the public and offering various incentives, you can attract a large number of small investments. This method not only provides financial support but also helps validate your product or service in the market.

3. Angel Investors: Angel investors are affluent individuals who provide capital to early-stage businesses in exchange for equity ownership. Many angel investors have a soft spot for veterans and actively seek investment opportunities in veteran-owned ventures. Networking through veteran entrepreneur organizations and pitch competitions can help you connect with potential angel investors.

4. Grants and Government Programs: There are numerous grants and government programs available specifically for veterans looking to start or expand their businesses. Research and tap into these resources, such as the SBA's Office of Veterans Business Development or the Department of Veterans Affairs' Veteran Entrepreneur Portal. These programs can provide not only financial support but also valuable mentorship and training.

5. Bootstrapping: If you have some personal savings or assets, you can consider self-funding your business. This approach allows you to maintain full control over your venture without incurring any debt. However, it may require a longer runway to reach profitability and can be risky if your personal finances are heavily tied to the success of the business.

As a veteran entrepreneur, it's essential to explore all available financing options and choose the ones that align with your business goals, risk tolerance, and personal circumstances. Remember, each option has its own pros and cons, and what works for one entrepreneur may not work for another. By combining multiple financing sources and utilizing your military background as a competitive advantage, you can secure the necessary funding to launch and grow your business.

Presenting a Compelling Business Case

Presenting a compelling business case is crucial for success. Whether you are a veteran, a business person, or a military personnel transitioning into entrepreneurship, mastering the art of presenting a persuasive business case is essential. This subchapter will provide you with valuable insights and strategies to captivate your audience and secure the support you need for your business venture.

As a veteran entrepreneur, you possess a unique set of skills and experiences that can greatly contribute to your business's success. However, effectively communicating these qualities can sometimes be a challenge. This subchapter will guide you through the process of crafting a business case that highlights your strengths and differentiates you from the competition.

First and foremost, it is important to clearly define your business idea and its potential value. Start by conducting thorough market research to identify your target audience, competitors, and industry trends. Use this information to develop a compelling value proposition that clearly articulates how your product or service solves a problem or fulfills a need better than others in the market.

Next, focus on establishing credibility and building trust. As a veteran, emphasize your military experience, which has instilled discipline, leadership, and resilience within you. Highlight how these qualities will translate into your business and reassure your audience that you are a reliable and trustworthy entrepreneur.

Furthermore, when presenting your business case, it is essential to support your claims with data and evidence. Utilize market research, industry statistics, and customer testimonials to back up your assertions and demonstrate the viability of your business idea. This will help you build a compelling argument and convince potential investors, partners, or customers to support your venture.

Lastly, remember the power of storytelling. As a veteran entrepreneur, you have a wealth of experiences that can resonate with your audience. Share your personal journey, the challenges you have overcome, and the lessons you have learned along the way. This will not only engage your audience emotionally but also demonstrate your determination and resilience.

Presenting a compelling business case is crucial for the success of any entrepreneur, particularly for veteran entrepreneurs who bring a unique set of skills and experiences to the table. By clearly defining your business idea, establishing credibility, providing evidence, and leveraging storytelling, you can captivate your audience and secure the support needed for your business venture. Embrace your warrior mindset and let it guide you towards business success.

Building Relationships with Investors and Lenders

In the journey of entrepreneurship, one of the most crucial aspects is undoubtedly securing funding to fuel your business venture. Whether you are a veteran or a business professional, understanding how to build relationships with investors and lenders is essential for your success. This subchapter aims to provide you with valuable insights and strategies to develop strong partnerships with these key stakeholders, ensuring the growth and sustainability of your business.

For veterans turned entrepreneurs, building relationships with investors and lenders can have unique challenges and advantages. Your military background instills discipline, resilience, and leadership skills, which can greatly benefit your entrepreneurial endeavors. Leverage these qualities to build trust and credibility with potential investors and lenders.

First and foremost, it is crucial to thoroughly research and understand the needs and preferences of your target investors and lenders. Tailor your pitch and business plan to align with their interests and goals. Present them with a compelling story that highlights your military experience, emphasizing how it translates into your business acumen and commitment to success.

Networking plays a pivotal role in building relationships with investors and lenders. Attend industry events, conferences, and seminars to connect with potential stakeholders. Join veteran entrepreneur networks and business organizations that cater to your niche. These platforms provide invaluable opportunities to meet like-minded individuals and establish meaningful connections.

Transparency and honesty are vital when dealing with investors and lenders. Clearly communicate your business goals, financial projections, and potential risks. Be prepared to answer questions and address concerns. Demonstrating integrity and trustworthiness will go a long way in building lasting relationships.

Additionally, consider seeking mentorship from experienced entrepreneurs or veterans who have successfully secured funding. Their guidance and insights can provide you with valuable advice and help you avoid common pitfalls.

Lastly, remember that building relationships with investors and lenders is a continuous process. Once you secure funding, maintain open lines of communication and keep them updated on your progress. Regularly assess the viability of your business model and make necessary adjustments to ensure the success of your venture.

Building relationships with investors and lenders is a critical aspect of entrepreneurship. For veterans turned entrepreneurs, their military background can provide a unique advantage in establishing trust and credibility. By leveraging networking opportunities, demonstrating transparency, and seeking mentorship, you can forge strong partnerships that will propel your business to new heights. Remember to maintain open communication and continuously evaluate your business model to ensure long-term success.

Chapter 5: Marketing and Branding Strategies

Developing a Strong Brand Identity

Establishing a strong brand identity is crucial for success. This subchapter aims to guide general readers, veterans, business people, and military personnel, especially those in the niche of the veteran entrepreneur, in understanding the importance of a robust brand identity and how to develop one.

A brand identity encompasses the values, personality, and purpose of a business. It is the perception customers have when they think of your company. For veteran entrepreneurs, leveraging their military experience can be a powerful tool in crafting a unique brand identity. By highlighting the values of discipline, integrity, and leadership acquired through military service, veterans can differentiate themselves from their competitors.

To develop a strong brand identity, it is essential to start by defining your target audience. Understanding the needs, desires, and pain points of your customers allows you to tailor your brand message and offerings to meet their expectations. For veterans, this could mean targeting clients who appreciate the values instilled in military personnel and seek to support them.

Consistency across all brand touch-points is crucial. From your logo to your website, social media presence, and customer interactions, every aspect of your brand should align with your core values and communicate a cohesive message. Veterans can showcase their military background through imagery, storytelling, or testimonials to build trust with their audience and establish credibility.

Authenticity is key. In a world saturated with marketing messages, consumers crave genuine connections. As a veteran entrepreneur, embracing your unique story and experiences will resonate with your target audience. Share how your military service has shaped your business philosophy, problem-solving skills, or dedication to customer satisfaction.

Leveraging digital platforms is vital for brand building in today's digital age. Utilize social media channels, blogs, and online communities to engage with your audience and share your brand's story. Share valuable content that educates, inspires, or entertains, while always staying true to your brand's voice and values.

Finally, consistently monitoring and adapting your brand strategy is essential for long-term success. Stay updated on industry trends, listen to customer feedback, and be open to evolving your brand identity as your business grows.

Developing a strong brand identity is a journey that requires time, effort, and continual refinement. For veteran entrepreneurs, it is an opportunity to leverage their unique experiences and values to create a powerful connection with their target audience. By defining their brand, staying consistent, and embracing authenticity, veteran entrepreneurs can build a brand that not only stands out but also resonates with their customers, driving business success.

Defining Your Brand Personality and Values

Establishing a strong and memorable brand is essential for success. Your brand is not just a logo or a catchy slogan; it is the essence of your business and what sets you apart from your competitors. As a veteran entrepreneur, you have a unique opportunity to leverage your military experience to create a brand that resonates with your target audience and reflects your values. This subchapter will guide you through the process of defining your brand personality and values, helping you craft a powerful and authentic brand that attracts customers and builds long-lasting relationships.

Your brand personality is the human characteristics and traits that your brand embodies. It is the way your brand speaks, behaves, and interacts with its audience. As a veteran entrepreneur, you have a wealth of experiences that can shape your brand personality. Consider the values and qualities that the military instilled in you – discipline, integrity, resilience, and teamwork, to name a few. How can you infuse these characteristics into your brand? Think about the tone of voice you want your brand to have, the emotions you want to evoke in your audience, and the overall impression you want to leave.

Defining your brand values is equally important. Your values are the principles and beliefs that guide your business decisions and actions. By clearly articulating your values, you not only attract like-minded customers but also create a strong internal culture within your business. As a veteran entrepreneur, you may already have a strong sense of values that you can translate into your brand. Perhaps you value service, loyalty, or innovation. These values can become the backbone of your brand and serve as a compass for decision-making.

To define your brand personality and values, start by conducting a self-assessment. Reflect on your military experience and the qualities that were most important to you during your service. Consider how these qualities can translate into your business and resonate with your target audience. Additionally, conduct market research to understand your customers' values and preferences. This will help you align your brand with their expectations and needs.

Once you have a clear understanding of your brand personality and values, you can begin to craft your brand identity. This includes creating a distinct visual identity, such as a logo, color palette, and typography that aligns with your brand personality. It also involves developing a consistent brand voice and messaging that reflects your values and resonates with your audience.

Remember, a strong brand is not built overnight. It requires consistent effort, authenticity, and ongoing refinement. By defining your brand personality and values, you can establish a powerful and memorable brand that sets you apart as a veteran entrepreneur and attracts customers who align with your mission and values.

Crafting a Memorable Brand Story

Having a memorable brand story is essential for success. It is especially crucial for veteran entrepreneurs who want to leverage their unique experiences and skill sets to build thriving businesses. Your brand story is what sets you apart from the crowd, captures the essence of your business, and resonates with your target audience. It is a powerful tool that can foster trust, loyalty, and a deep connection with your customers. In this chapter, we will explore the key elements of crafting a memorable brand story that will leave a lasting impression.

1. Embrace Your Military Background: As a veteran entrepreneur, your military service is an integral part of your brand story. Highlight how your experiences have shaped your values, work ethic, and problem-solving skills. This will not only differentiate you from your competitors but also appeal to a niche audience of fellow veterans who value the military mindset.

2. Identify Your Unique Selling Proposition: Determine what sets your business apart from others in your industry. Is it your expertise, innovative approach, or commitment to exceptional customer service?

Clearly communicate this unique selling proposition in your brand story to showcase what makes your business stand out.

3. Connect Emotionally: People connect with stories that evoke emotions. Share personal anecdotes that demonstrate the challenges you've overcome and how your business solves a problem or fulfills a need. This emotional connection will help your audience relate to your brand and build trust.

4. Be Authentic and Transparent: Authenticity is key in building a brand that resonates with your audience. Be true to your values, mission, and vision. Transparency is also crucial in establishing trust. Share your successes, failures, and lessons learned along your entrepreneurial journey.

5. Consistency is Key: A memorable brand story should be consistent across all your marketing channels. From your website to social media platforms, ensure that your brand story is compelling, cohesive, and aligned with your overall brand identity.

6. Engage with Your Audience: Encourage your audience to interact with your brand story. Create opportunities for them to share their own stories, provide feedback, or engage in conversations. This two-way communication will deepen the connection and loyalty between your brand and your audience.

Crafting a memorable brand story is a vital aspect of building a successful business as a veteran entrepreneur. By embracing your military background, identifying your unique selling proposition, connecting emotionally, being authentic and transparent, maintaining consistency, and engaging with your audience, you can create a brand story that leaves a lasting impression. Your brand story will not only attract customers but also build a community of loyal supporters who believe in your mission and values.

Establishing Brand Guidelines and Consistency

In a competitive business landscape, a strong and consistent brand is essential for success. Whether you are a veteran entrepreneur or a business professional, understanding the importance of brand guidelines and consistency can make a significant difference in your company's growth and recognition.

Brand guidelines are a set of rules that define how your brand should be presented to the world. They encompass everything from your logo and color palette to your tone of voice and overall brand personality. By establishing brand guidelines, you ensure that your brand remains cohesive and easily recognizable across all platforms and touch-points.

For veterans venturing into entrepreneurship, brand guidelines can be particularly valuable. Your military background gives you a unique perspective and story to share with your audience, and your brand should reflect that. By defining your brand's values, mission, and voice, you can create a strong connection with your target audience, which may include other veterans, businesspeople, and military personnel.

Consistency plays a vital role in establishing a strong brand presence. When your audience sees your brand consistently represented in a certain way, it builds trust and familiarity. This is especially important for veterans in business, as you want to be seen as a reliable and credible source.

To ensure consistency throughout your brand, it is crucial to implement your guidelines across all communication channels. This includes your website, social media profiles, marketing materials, and even your personal interactions with clients and customers. By doing so, you reinforce your brand's identity and make it easier for your target audience to connect with you.

Moreover, consistency in branding helps you stand out from the competition. In a crowded marketplace, having a unique and recognizable brand can give you a competitive edge. By consistently following your brand guidelines, you create a memorable impression that differentiates you from others in your niche.

Establishing brand guidelines and consistency is crucial for the success of any business, especially for veteran entrepreneurs. By defining your brand's values, mission, and voice, and implementing these guidelines consistently across all touch-points, you can create a strong and recognizable brand that resonates with your target audience. This will not only build trust and credibility but also help you stand out in a crowded marketplace. So, take the time to establish your brand guidelines and ensure that your brand remains consistent in its representation.

Effective Marketing Techniques

Effective marketing techniques are essential for success. Whether you are a general reader, a veteran, a business person, or a military personnel interested in entrepreneurship, understanding how to effectively market your products or services is crucial to achieving your goals. This subchapter titled "Effective Marketing Techniques" from the book "Warrior Mindset, Business Success: A Veteran's Guide to Entrepreneurship" will equip you with valuable insights and strategies to navigate the complex marketing landscape.

Marketing is not just about advertising; it encompasses a wide range of activities aimed at promoting your brand, attracting customers, and increasing sales. In this subchapter, we will explore proven marketing techniques that are tailored specifically for veteran entrepreneurs. Drawing on the unique experiences and skills that veterans possess, we will delve into strategies that leverage your military background to differentiate your business from competitors.

One of the key aspects of effective marketing is understanding your target audience. We will discuss how to identify and define your target market, allowing you to tailor your marketing efforts to resonate with your ideal customers. Additionally, we will delve into market research, helping you uncover valuable insights about your industry, competitors, and customer preferences.

Another crucial element of effective marketing is creating a compelling brand identity. We will explore the importance of branding and how to develop a brand that reflects your values, mission, and vision. Through case studies and real-world examples, you will learn how to establish a strong brand presence that builds trust and loyalty among your customers.

Furthermore, we will dive into various marketing channels and strategies, including digital marketing, social media marketing, content marketing, and influencer marketing. These techniques will equip you with the tools to reach your target audience effectively and maximize your marketing efforts within your budget.

Lastly, we will discuss how to measure the success of your marketing campaigns and make data-driven decisions. By analyzing key metrics and tracking the return on investment of your marketing efforts, you will be able to refine your strategies and optimize your marketing budget for better results.

Whether you are a veteran entrepreneur looking to take your business to the next level or a general reader interested in effective marketing techniques, this subchapter will empower you with the knowledge and skills necessary to thrive in the competitive business landscape. By implementing these proven marketing techniques, you will gain a competitive edge, attract more customers, and ultimately achieve long-term business success.

Identifying Target Markets and Customer Segments

Understanding your target market and identifying customer segments is crucial for business success. This subchapter aims to guide general audiences, veterans, business people, and military personnel through the process of identifying their target markets and customer segments, with a specific focus on the niche of the veteran entrepreneur.

As a veteran entrepreneur, you possess a unique set of skills and experiences that can be leveraged to your advantage. However, to effectively reach your intended audience, you must first identify who they are and what their specific needs and preferences are.

The first step in identifying your target market is conducting thorough market research. This involves gathering data and insights about your industry, competitors, and potential customers. By analyzing market trends, consumer behaviors, and competitor strategies, you can gain valuable insights into your target market.

For the veteran entrepreneur niche, it is important to understand the specific challenges and opportunities that veterans face when transitioning into entrepreneurship. This could include factors such as limited access to capital, a desire for a sense of purpose, and a preference for working in a team-oriented environment. By understanding these unique characteristics, you can tailor your products or services to meet the specific needs of this niche audience.

Once you have identified your target market, it is essential to segment your customers based on their characteristics, preferences, and buying behaviors. This segmentation allows you to create tailored marketing strategies and messages that resonate with each customer segment. For the veteran entrepreneur niche, you may have segments such as recently transitioned veterans, disabled veterans, or veterans seeking to start social impact businesses.

To effectively reach your target market and customer segments, it is important to utilize various marketing channels and tactics. This could include digital marketing strategies such as social media advertising, content marketing, and search engine optimization. Additionally, networking events, industry conferences, and partnerships with veteran organizations can also help increase your visibility and reach within the veteran entrepreneur community.

Identifying target markets and customer segments is a critical step in the journey towards entrepreneurial success. By understanding the unique characteristics and needs of the veteran entrepreneur niche, you can tailor your products, services, and marketing strategies to effectively reach and serve this audience. Remember, success lies in understanding your customers and providing them with valuable solutions that meet their specific needs.

Creating a Comprehensive Marketing Plan

Having a well-defined marketing plan is crucial for the success of any venture. This subchapter, "Creating a Comprehensive Marketing Plan," from the book "Warrior Mindset: A Veteran's Guide to Entrepreneurship and Business" offers a step-by-step guide to help general readers, veterans, business people, and military personnel in the niche of the veteran entrepreneur develop an effective marketing strategy.

A comprehensive marketing plan lays the foundation for attracting customers, building brand awareness, and ultimately driving sales. It begins with a thorough understanding of your target audience, market research, and competitor analysis. By identifying your ideal customer and studying market trends, you can tailor your marketing efforts to resonate with your target market.

Once you have defined your target audience, the next step is to establish your marketing objectives. What do you aim to achieve through your marketing efforts? Are you looking to increase brand awareness, generate leads, or boost sales? Setting clear and measurable goals will enable you to track your progress and evaluate the success of your marketing plan.

The subchapter also delves into various marketing strategies that can be employed to reach your target audience effectively. It covers both traditional and digital marketing techniques, including advertising, public relations, social media marketing, content marketing, and search engine optimization (SEO). By combining different marketing channels, you can create a multi-faceted approach that maximizes your reach and engagement.

Furthermore, the subchapter emphasizes the importance of developing a strong brand identity and consistent messaging across all marketing platforms. Your brand represents your company's values, mission, and unique selling proposition. By effectively communicating your brand message and value proposition, you can differentiate yourself from competitors and establish credibility in the market.

Lastly, the subchapter provides guidance on tracking and analyzing the effectiveness of your marketing efforts. By leveraging various analytics tools, you can gain valuable insights into customer behavior, campaign performance, and return on investment (ROI). This data-driven approach enables you to make informed decisions and optimize your marketing strategy for maximum impact.

In conclusion, "Creating a Comprehensive Marketing Plan" offers a comprehensive roadmap to help general readers, veterans, business people, and military personnel in the niche of the veteran entrepreneur develop a robust marketing strategy. By understanding your target audience, setting clear objectives, employing various marketing techniques, and analyzing data, you can create a marketing plan that drives business success and propels your venture forward.

Leveraging Digital Marketing Channels

Digital marketing has become an essential tool for businesses to thrive and succeed. The rapid advancements in technology have opened up new avenues and opportunities for entrepreneurs, including veterans, to promote their products or services effectively. This subchapter will explore the various digital marketing channels available and how they can be leveraged to maximize business success for the veteran entrepreneur.

One of the most popular and widely used digital marketing channels is social media. Platforms such as Facebook, Instagram, Twitter, and LinkedIn offer a vast audience reach and the ability to engage directly with potential customers. The veteran entrepreneur can utilize these platforms to create brand awareness, foster customer loyalty, and generate leads. By sharing compelling content, engaging in conversations, and running targeted ads, veterans can effectively leverage social media for their business growth.

Another powerful digital marketing channel is search engine optimization (SEO). By optimizing their website and content for search engines, veteran entrepreneurs can ensure that their business appears prominently in search engine results, driving organic traffic to their website. Utilizing SEO techniques such as keyword research, on-page optimization, and link building, veterans can enhance their online visibility and attract potential customers who are actively searching for their products or services.

Email marketing is another effective digital marketing strategy that veterans can leverage to connect with their target audience. By building an email list and nurturing it with valuable content and offers, veterans can establish a direct line of communication with their customers. Through personalized and targeted email campaigns, the veteran entrepreneur can drive customer engagement, promote new products or services, and ultimately increase sales and customer loyalty.

Furthermore, content marketing plays a crucial role in digital marketing. By creating and sharing relevant and valuable content, veterans can position themselves as industry experts and thought leaders. Through blog posts, articles, videos, podcasts, and infographics, they can educate and inspire their target audience, building trust and credibility. Content marketing not only drives organic traffic but also helps establish long-term relationships with customers.

Leveraging digital marketing channels is essential for the success of the veteran entrepreneur. By utilizing social media, search engine optimization, email marketing, and content marketing, veterans can effectively reach and engage with their target audience, drive traffic to their website, and ultimately grow their business. Embracing these digital marketing strategies will empower veterans to navigate the competitive business landscape and achieve their entrepreneurial goals.

Chapter 6: Sales and Customer Relationship Management

B uilding and Managing a Sales Team

Building and managing a sales team is essential for the success of any business. In this subchapter, we will explore the key strategies and principles that veterans, business people, and military personnel can apply to effectively build and manage a sales team.

First and foremost, it is crucial to recognize the importance of hiring the right individuals for your sales team. As a veteran entrepreneur, you possess unique qualities and experiences that can be invaluable in identifying suitable candidates. Look for individuals who embody the warrior mindset – those who are disciplined, resilient, and possess a strong work ethic. Hiring people who share your values and vision will contribute to a cohesive and motivated team.

Once you have assembled your sales team, effective management is crucial. Establish clear goals and expectations, and provide your team with the resources and support they need to succeed. As a veteran, you understand the significance of effective communication and teamwork. Encourage open and honest communication within your team, fostering an environment where ideas and feedback can be freely shared.

In order to maximize the potential of your sales team, ongoing training and development are vital. Provide your team with the necessary tools and training to enhance their skills and knowledge. This could include sales techniques, product knowledge, or customer relationship management. By investing in the growth and development of your sales team, you are investing in the future success of your business.

Motivation is another key element to consider when managing a sales team. As a veteran entrepreneur, you possess the leadership skills necessary to inspire and motivate your team. Recognize and reward their achievements, and create a positive and supportive work culture. By fostering a sense of camaraderie and celebrating both individual and team successes, you will cultivate a motivated and driven sales team.

Lastly, it is important to continually evaluate the performance and progress of your sales team. Implement metrics and performance indicators to track their success and identify areas for improvement. Regularly review and provide constructive feedback to your team members, helping them to grow and reach their full potential.

Building and managing a sales team requires careful consideration and effective leadership. By hiring the right individuals, providing training and support, motivating your team, and continually evaluating their performance, you can build a successful sales team that drives the growth and success of your business. As a veteran entrepreneur, you possess the warrior mindset necessary to excel in this endeavor. Embrace the challenge and lead your sales team to victory.

Recruiting and Training Sales Professionals

In the world of business, sales professionals play a critical role in driving revenue and ensuring the success of a company. For veteran entrepreneurs, understanding the importance of recruiting and training top-notch sales professionals can make all the difference in achieving business success. In this subchapter, we will delve into the essential strategies and tactics for recruiting and training sales professionals, specifically tailored to the needs and experiences of the veteran entrepreneur.

Recruiting the right sales professionals is the first step towards building a powerful sales team. As a veteran entrepreneur, you possess unique qualities and experiences that can greatly benefit your recruitment process. Leveraging your military background, you can identify candidates who possess the necessary traits such as discipline, resilience, and a strong work ethic. Additionally, networking within veteran communities and utilizing online platforms that cater to veterans can provide access to a pool of talented individuals who understand the value of teamwork and commitment.

Once you have successfully recruited sales professionals, it is crucial to provide them with comprehensive training to ensure they are equipped with the skills and knowledge required to excel in their roles. Drawing on your own experience in the military, you can develop a structured training program that focuses on building effective communication skills, negotiation techniques, and product knowledge. Incorporating real-life scenarios and role-playing exercises can help sales professionals develop the confidence and adaptability necessary to thrive in a competitive business environment.

Furthermore, as a veteran entrepreneur, you have the advantage of understanding the importance of leadership and mentorship. Take the time to establish a supportive and collaborative culture within your sales team. Encourage open communication, provide ongoing feedback, and foster an environment that promotes continuous learning and professional growth. By creating a sense of camaraderie and shared purpose, you can motivate and inspire your sales professionals to achieve exceptional results.

Recruiting and training sales professionals is a critical aspect of business success for veteran entrepreneurs. By leveraging your military background, networking within veteran communities, and implementing a comprehensive training program, you can build a high-performing sales team that drives revenue and propels your business forward. Remember, as a veteran entrepreneur, you possess unique qualities and experiences that can greatly contribute to the success of your sales team. Embrace your warrior mindset and lead your sales professionals towards victory in the competitive world of business.

Setting Sales Targets and Incentives

In any business, setting sales targets and incentives is crucial for driving growth and success. This subchapter will explore the importance of setting sales targets and how they can be effectively used to motivate and incentivize sales teams. It is specifically tailored to the needs and experiences of Veteran entrepreneurs, combining military discipline and business acumen to achieve optimal results.

The first step in setting sales targets is to establish clear, measurable goals. This involves analyzing past performance, market trends, and the specific objectives of the business. Veterans, with their strong analytical skills and attention to detail, are well-equipped to carry out this crucial task. By setting realistic and attainable targets, entrepreneurs can ensure their sales teams are focused and motivated to achieve them.

Once the targets are set, it is vital to communicate them effectively to the sales team. Veterans, with their exceptional communication skills developed during their military service, can effectively convey expectations and motivate their teams towards the desired outcomes. By clearly outlining the targets and explaining their importance, entrepreneurs can foster a sense of purpose and drive among their sales personnel.

To further incentivize the team, it is essential to design a comprehensive rewards program. Veterans, having experienced the power of recognition and rewards in the military, understand the importance of acknowledging outstanding performance. By offering incentives such as bonuses, commissions, or recognition programs, entrepreneurs can provide tangible rewards for achieving or surpassing sales targets. This not only motivates the team but also creates healthy competition and camaraderie among sales professionals.

However, it is important to strike a balance between setting challenging targets and ensuring they are attainable. Unrealistic or overly ambitious targets can demotivate sales teams and lead to burnout. Veterans, having experienced the challenges of mission planning and execution, are well-versed in finding this delicate balance. By leveraging their skills, entrepreneurs can set targets that push their teams to excel without overwhelming them.

Setting sales targets and incentives is vital for business success, and Veteran entrepreneurs bring a unique perspective to this process. By combining their military discipline, strong analytical skills, and effective communication abilities, they can establish realistic targets, motivate sales teams, and design comprehensive rewards programs. This subchapter serves as a practical guide for Veteran entrepreneurs seeking to maximize their sales performance and drive their business towards prosperity.

Monitoring Performance and Providing Feedback

Monitoring performance and providing feedback is a crucial aspect of achieving success. Whether you are a general audience member, a veteran, a business person, or a military personnel looking to venture into entrepreneurship, understanding how to effectively monitor performance and provide feedback is essential for your journey as a veteran entrepreneur.

As a veteran entrepreneur, you bring a unique set of skills and experiences to the business world. Your military background has equipped you with discipline, determination, and the ability to adapt to challenging situations. However, to excel in the competitive business landscape, it is important to establish a system to monitor your performance and continually improve.

One effective way to monitor performance is by setting measurable goals and key performance indicators (KPIs). These goals and KPIs should be specific, attainable, and time-bound. By regularly tracking your progress against these metrics, you can identify areas of improvement and make necessary adjustments to your business strategies.

Feedback is another crucial element in monitoring performance and driving growth. As a veteran entrepreneur, it is important to create an environment that encourages open and honest communication. Regularly seeking feedback from your team, customers, and mentors can provide valuable insights into areas where you can enhance your performance.

When providing feedback, it is important to focus on both positive reinforcement and constructive criticism. Recognize and celebrate successes, as this will motivate your team and instill a sense of accomplishment. However, do not shy away from addressing areas that need improvement. Constructive feedback should be specific, actionable, and delivered in a respectful manner.

In addition to seeking feedback externally, it is crucial to develop self-awareness and engage in self-reflection. Take the time to evaluate your own performance, strengths, and weaknesses. This introspection will enable you to identify areas where you can grow and develop as a veteran entrepreneur.

Furthermore, leveraging technology can greatly aid in monitoring performance and providing feedback. There are numerous tools and software available that can track various business metrics, automate reporting, and provide real-time insights. Embracing these technological advancements can help you make informed decisions and stay ahead of the competition.

Monitoring performance and providing feedback are essential components of success for veteran entrepreneurs. By setting measurable goals, seeking feedback, and leveraging technology, you can continuously monitor and improve your performance. Remember, as a veteran entrepreneur, your military background has equipped you with a warrior mindset – a mindset that allows you to overcome any challenge and achieve success in the business world.

Developing Strong Customer Relationships

Building and maintaining strong customer relationships is essential for long-term success. This holds true for all entrepreneurs, but particularly for those who have served in the military and are now venturing into the world of business as veteran entrepreneurs. In this subchapter, we will explore the importance of developing strong customer relationships and provide practical strategies to help veterans succeed in this area.

As veterans, you possess unique qualities that can greatly contribute to your success as entrepreneurs. Traits such as discipline, integrity, and a strong work ethic are highly valued in both the military and business worlds. However, it is equally important to recognize and embrace the need for effective communication and relationship-building skills when transitioning to the business sector.

Building strong customer relationships starts with understanding your target audience. As a veteran entrepreneur, you have the advantage of a shared experience with other veterans. This shared experience can be leveraged to establish rapport and trust with potential customers who are also veterans. By understanding their needs, challenges, and aspirations, you can tailor your products or services to better meet their specific requirements.

Moreover, effective communication is key to establishing and maintaining strong customer relationships. Veterans are known for their ability to communicate concisely and effectively. However, it is important to adapt your communication style to fit the business context. This includes active listening, understanding nonverbal cues, and using appropriate language to connect with your customers.

Another crucial aspect of developing strong customer relationships as a veteran entrepreneur is providing exceptional customer service. Veterans are accustomed to going above and beyond in their duties, and this mentality should extend to the way you interact with your customers. Responding promptly to inquiries, resolving issues with empathy and professionalism, and consistently delivering on your promises will help you build trust and loyalty among your customer base.

Finally, leveraging technology and digital platforms can be a game-changer for veteran entrepreneurs in developing strong customer relationships. Utilizing social media, email marketing, and customer relationship management (CRM) systems can help you stay connected with your customers, understand their preferences, and personalize your interactions.

Developing strong customer relationships is vital for the success of veteran entrepreneurs. By leveraging your unique qualities, understanding your target audience, communicating effectively, providing exceptional customer service, and utilizing technology, you can establish and maintain lasting relationships with your customers. These relationships will not only contribute to your business success but also create a sense of camaraderie and trust, aligning with the values ingrained in the military community.

Understanding Customer Needs and Preferences

In entrepreneurship and business, success hinges on a deep understanding of customer needs and preferences. Whether you are a veteran starting your own business or a seasoned entrepreneur, this subchapter aims to equip you with the knowledge and strategies necessary to build a customer-centric business and gain a competitive edge.

As a veteran entrepreneur, you possess unique qualities that can set you apart in the business world. Your military background has instilled in you discipline, dedication, and a keen ability to adapt to challenging situations. Now, it is time to leverage these skills to understand and meet the needs of your customers effectively.

To begin, it is essential to conduct thorough market research. This involves analyzing your target audience, identifying their pain points, and uncovering their preferences. By understanding your customers' needs, you can tailor your products or services to offer solutions that resonate with them.

One effective strategy is to create customer personas. These personas represent fictional characters that embody the traits and characteristics of your target customers. By personifying your customers, you can gain a deeper understanding of their demographics, interests, and motivations, enabling you to tailor your offerings to suit their preferences.

Another key aspect of understanding customer needs is actively listening to their feedback. Encourage your customers to provide feedback through surveys, social media, or face-to-face interactions. This feedback can provide invaluable insights into how your products or services are perceived and help you identify areas for improvement.

Moreover, cultivating strong relationships with your customers is crucial. Building trust and loyalty can be achieved through exceptional customer service, personalized experiences, and consistent communication. By fostering a customer-centric culture within your business, you can create a strong bond with your target audience, resulting in repeat business and positive word-of-mouth referrals.

Understanding customer needs and preferences is a fundamental aspect of building a successful business. As a veteran entrepreneur, your unique background and skills can give you a competitive advantage in this endeavor. By conducting thorough market research, creating customer personas, actively listening to feedback, and cultivating strong relationships with your customers, you can develop a customer-centric business that meets and exceeds their expectations. Remember, a satisfied customer is not just a one-time sale but a long-term advocate for your brand.

Providing Excellent Customer Service

Providing excellent customer service has become a crucial aspect for any successful venture. Whether you are a veteran entrepreneur or a business person from any background, understanding the importance of customer service and implementing effective strategies is paramount. This subchapter will delve into the key principles and strategies that can help you deliver exceptional customer service, fostering loyalty, and driving business success.

1. The Customer-Centric Approach:

To excel in customer service, it is essential to adopt a customer-centric mindset. Recognize that your customers are the lifeblood of your business and prioritize their needs and satisfaction above all else. By understanding their pain points, preferences, and expectations, you can tailor your products or services to meet and exceed their requirements.

2. Building Strong Relationships:

Establishing and nurturing strong relationships with your customers is vital. Focus on creating a positive and memorable experience at every touchpoint. This includes providing prompt responses, personalized interactions, and going the extra mile to address their concerns. By building trust and rapport, you can cultivate loyal customers who will become ambassadors for your brand.

3. Effective Communication:

Clear and effective communication is the cornerstone of exceptional customer service. Ensure that your team is well-trained in communication skills, both verbal and written, to effectively convey information, address queries, and resolve complaints. Active listening is also crucial to understand your customers' needs fully.

4. Continuous Improvement:

Strive for continuous improvement by regularly seeking feedback from your customers. Conduct surveys, ask for reviews, and monitor social media platforms to gauge customer satisfaction and identify areas for enhancement. By constantly refining your processes and offerings based on customer feedback, you can stay ahead of the competition and provide an exceptional experience.

5. Empowering Your Team:

Your team plays a significant role in delivering excellent customer service. Empower them with the knowledge, tools, and autonomy to make decisions and resolve customer issues promptly. Invest in training programs to enhance their skills and encourage a customer-centric mindset throughout your organization.

Remember, providing excellent customer service is not just about resolving complaints; it is about building relationships, exceeding expectations, and creating a positive brand image. By implementing these strategies, you can differentiate yourself in the market, attract loyal customers, and achieve long-term business success.

Whether you are a military personnel transitioning into entrepreneurship or a business person looking to enhance customer service, mastering this aspect is vital. By adopting the principles outlined in this subchapter, you can elevate your customer service game and propel your business to new heights.

Retaining and Upselling to Existing Customers

It is easy to get caught up in the constant pursuit of new customers. However, as a veteran entrepreneur, you understand the importance of loyalty and building strong relationships. Retaining and upselling to existing customers should be a top priority for your business.

Why is it crucial to focus on retaining and upselling to existing customers? Well, for starters, it is much more cost-effective than acquiring new customers. Studies have shown that it costs five times more to attract a new customer than to keep an existing one. Furthermore, existing customers are more likely to make repeat purchases and spend more money with your business.

As a veteran, you already possess the discipline and dedication needed to excel in this area. Here are some strategies to help you retain and upsell to your existing customer base:

1. Provide exceptional customer service: Make your customers feel valued and appreciated by going above and beyond their expectations. Respond promptly to their inquiries and concerns, and always strive to exceed their needs.

2. Personalize your approach: Take the time to understand your customers' preferences, needs, and pain points. Tailor your products or services to address their specific requirements, and communicate with them in a way that resonates with their individual personalities.

3. Offer loyalty programs and incentives: Show your appreciation for your customers' continued support by offering exclusive benefits, discounts, or rewards for their loyalty. Encourage them to refer your business to others by providing incentives for successful referrals.

4. Regularly communicate and engage: Stay top-of-mind by communicating with your customers regularly. This can be through email newsletters, social media updates, or personalized messages. Engage with them by asking for feedback, sharing useful information, or inviting them to exclusive events.

5. Upsell and cross-sell strategically: Take advantage of the trust and rapport you have built with your existing customers to upsell or cross-sell complementary products or services. This not only increases your revenue but also adds value to their overall experience.

Remember, retaining and upselling to existing customers is an ongoing process. Continually monitor their satisfaction, adapt your strategies, and consistently deliver exceptional value. By prioritizing your existing customer base, you will build a loyal following and create a strong foundation for long-term business success.

Whether you are a veteran, a business person, or military personnel, implementing these strategies will help you maintain a thriving business and establish yourself as a trusted entrepreneur in your niche.

Chapter 7: Scaling and Growth Strategies

Identifying Opportunities for Growth

Identifying opportunities for growth is essential for success. This holds true for everyone, regardless of their background or industry. However, for veterans transitioning into entrepreneurship, this process may seem daunting at first. That is why this subchapter aims to provide valuable insights and guidance to help veterans, business people, and military personnel recognize and seize opportunities for growth.

As a veteran entrepreneur, you possess unique skills and experiences that can give you a competitive edge in the business world. Your military training has instilled in you a warrior mindset, characterized by discipline, resilience, and adaptability. These qualities can be leveraged to identify and capitalize on opportunities that others might overlook.

One strategy for identifying opportunities for growth is to stay informed about industry trends. By keeping a close eye on market developments, emerging technologies, and consumer preferences, you can spot gaps or areas of improvement within your niche. This allows you to tailor your products or services to meet the evolving needs of your target audience, positioning yourself as an industry leader.

Networking also plays a vital role in identifying growth opportunities. As a veteran, you have a vast network of fellow servicemen and women, mentors, and business contacts. Engaging with these individuals can provide valuable insights, partnerships, and referrals that can open doors to new opportunities. Attend industry conferences, join professional associations, and actively participate in online communities to expand your network and stay connected with the latest industry trends.

Furthermore, embracing innovation and technology can be a game-changer for your business. Explore how you can leverage digital platforms, automation, and data analytics to streamline your operations, enhance customer experience, and identify untapped markets. By staying open to new technologies and continuously seeking ways to improve your business processes, you can position yourself for long-term growth and success.

Identifying opportunities for growth is a crucial aspect of entrepreneurship. As a veteran entrepreneur, you possess a unique set of skills and experiences that can help you excel in this area. By staying informed, networking, and embracing innovation, you can position yourself at the forefront of your industry, drive sustainable growth, and achieve business success.

Assessing Market Trends and Demand

Staying ahead of market trends and understanding consumer demand is crucial for success. This subchapter delves into the importance of assessing market trends and demand, particularly for the veteran entrepreneur. Whether you are a general reader, a veteran, a business person, or a military personnel, this chapter will equip you with valuable insights to navigate the ever-changing business landscape.

As a veteran entrepreneur, you possess a unique set of skills and experiences that can give you a competitive edge. However, it is essential to adapt and understand the market trends relevant to your industry. By analyzing market trends, you can identify opportunities, anticipate changes, and position your business for growth.

Assessing market trends starts with conducting thorough research. This involves studying industry reports, monitoring competitor activities, and staying updated with the latest news and developments. By immersing yourself in the market, you can identify emerging trends, consumer preferences, and potential gaps in the market.

Understanding consumer demand is equally important. By examining consumer behavior, you can align your offerings with their needs and preferences. Conduct surveys, interviews, or focus groups to gather insights directly from your target audience. This information will help you refine your products or services and create a compelling value proposition.

Furthermore, technology plays a significant role in assessing market trends and demand. Leverage digital tools and analytics to gather and analyze data efficiently. Social media platforms, online surveys, and web analytics can provide valuable information about your target market, allowing you to make informed business decisions.

In addition to gathering data, networking and building relationships with industry professionals can provide invaluable insights into market trends. Attend trade shows, join industry associations, and participate in networking events to connect with like-minded entrepreneurs and stay informed about the latest trends and developments in your field.

Lastly, remain adaptable and open to change. Markets are dynamic, and trends can shift rapidly. Regularly reassess your strategies, evaluate your competitors, and listen to feedback from your customers. Embrace innovation and be ready to pivot when necessary.

Assessing market trends and demand is a fundamental aspect of entrepreneurship, especially for veteran entrepreneurs. By conducting thorough research, understanding consumer preferences, leveraging technology, networking, and remaining adaptable, you can stay ahead of the game and position your business for long-term success. Embrace the warrior mindset and let it guide you in navigating the challenges and opportunities of the business world.

Exploring Expansion Strategies

Growth and expansion are crucial for long-term success. As a veteran entrepreneur, you possess a unique set of skills and experiences that can be leveraged to drive growth and take your business to new heights. In this subchapter, we will delve into various expansion strategies that you can consider to propel your business forward.

1. Diversify your product/service offerings: One way to expand your business is to diversify your product or service offerings. Identify gaps in the market and evaluate how your skills and expertise can be utilized to meet those needs. By offering a broader range of products or services, you can attract new customers and increase revenue streams.

2. Enter new markets: Expanding into new markets can open up a world of opportunities for your business. Consider conducting market research to identify potential markets that align with your business goals and target audience. Develop a market entry strategy that takes into account the cultural, economic, and regulatory aspects of the new market.

3. Form strategic partnerships: Collaborating with other businesses or organizations can be an effective way to expand your reach and customer base. Look for strategic partnerships that can complement your offerings and provide mutual benefits. By leveraging each other's networks and resources, you can tap into new markets and increase brand visibility.

4. Franchising or licensing: If your business model can be replicated, franchising or licensing can be a viable expansion strategy. This allows

you to expand your brand presence without bearing the entire burden of opening new locations. However, thorough planning, documentation, and legal considerations are essential before embarking on this path.

5. Online presence and e-commerce: In today's digital age, having a strong online presence is crucial for business growth. Invest in building a user-friendly website, optimize it for search engines, and leverage social media platforms to reach a wider audience. Consider incorporating e-commerce capabilities to tap into the growing online consumer market.

6. Acquisitions or mergers: For rapid expansion, acquiring or merging with complementary businesses can be a powerful strategy. Identify potential targets that align with your business goals and conduct thorough due diligence before proceeding. This strategy allows you to gain access to new customers, technologies, or geographic markets.

Remember, expansion requires careful planning, resource allocation, and risk management. Assess the scalability of your business model and evaluate the financial implications of each expansion strategy. Leverage your military training, discipline, and adaptability to navigate the challenges that come with growth. With the right mindset and strategic approach, you can successfully expand your business and achieve long-term success as a veteran entrepreneur.

Evaluating Risks and Mitigation Plans

Evaluating risks and implementing effective mitigation plans is crucial for any entrepreneur, especially for those who have served in the military. This subchapter aims to provide valuable insights and strategies for veterans venturing into entrepreneurship, as well as business professionals and military personnel seeking guidance on risk management.

Veterans possess a unique set of skills and experiences that can be leveraged to excel in the business world. However, adapting to the civilian business environment requires a keen understanding of risk assessment and mitigation. This subchapter will outline the key steps to evaluating risks and developing robust mitigation plans, ensuring a successful transition into the world of entrepreneurship.

Firstly, understanding the potential risks involved in any business endeavor is essential. This includes identifying both internal and external risks, such as financial uncertainties, market volatility, competition, and unforeseen events. Veterans, with their military background, are adept at analyzing and assessing risks, making them well-equipped for this crucial task.

Once risks are identified, the next step is to develop effective mitigation plans. This involves creating strategies to minimize the likelihood of risks occurring and to lessen their impact if they do. Veterans can draw upon their problem-solving skills and ability to think on their feet to devise innovative and proactive solutions. Additionally, the subchapter will provide practical examples and case studies that highlight successful risk mitigation strategies employed by veteran entrepreneurs.

Furthermore, the subchapter will emphasize the importance of continuous monitoring and reassessment of risks and mitigation plans. The business landscape is constantly evolving, and what may have been an effective mitigation plan yesterday may not be sufficient today. Veterans, with their disciplined approach and adaptability, will find this aspect of risk management particularly valuable.

In summary, evaluating risks and mitigation plans is a vital resource for veterans transitioning into entrepreneurship, as well as for business professionals and military personnel seeking to enhance their risk management skills. By utilizing their military experience and combining it with the principles outlined in this subchapter, veterans can develop a warrior mindset for business success. With a thorough understanding of risk evaluation, effective mitigation planning, and continuous monitoring, veteran entrepreneurs can confidently navigate the challenges of entrepreneurship and achieve their business goals.

Managing Change and Adaptability

Change is an inevitable part of life, and it is especially crucial in the world of business and entrepreneurship. In today's fast-paced and dynamic marketplace, those who can effectively manage change and adapt to new circumstances are the ones who thrive. This subchapter explores the importance of managing change and adaptability, with a particular focus on the unique challenges and opportunities faced by veteran entrepreneurs.

As veterans, you have already demonstrated your ability to adapt and overcome adversity in the military. The same principles apply to the business world. Change can come in many forms, from shifts in the market to new technologies and customer demands. Being able to quickly identify and embrace change is essential for staying competitive and growing your business.

One of the key aspects of managing change is having a growth mindset. This means seeing challenges as opportunities for learning and growth rather than as obstacles. As a veteran entrepreneur, you have already cultivated a mindset of resilience and perseverance. By harnessing these qualities, you can approach change with a positive attitude and the belief that you can overcome any obstacles that come your way.

Another crucial factor in managing change is staying informed and continuously learning. The business landscape is constantly evolving, and it is essential to stay up-to-date with industry trends, new technologies, and best practices. As a veteran, you have a natural inclination towards self-improvement and a thirst for knowledge. By actively seeking out new information and learning opportunities, you can position yourself as a leader in your field and adapt quickly to change.

In addition to personal growth, building a network of support is vital for managing change. Surrounding yourself with like-minded individuals, mentors, and fellow veteran entrepreneurs can provide a valuable source of guidance and encouragement. By tapping into the collective wisdom and experiences of your network, you can gain valuable insights and perspectives on managing change and adapting to new circumstances.

Lastly, it is essential to be open-minded and agile in your decision-making process. Veteran entrepreneurs often have a structured and disciplined approach to problem-solving, which can be a tremendous asset. However, it is also essential to be flexible and willing to adjust your strategies based on new information and market conditions. Embracing change and adaptability means being willing to let go of old ways of doing things and embracing new and innovative approaches.

Managing change and adaptability is crucial for success in business, and this holds especially true for veteran entrepreneurs. By adopting a growth mindset, continuously learning, building a network of support, and being open-minded, you can navigate change with confidence and embrace the opportunities that come with it. Your military background has already equipped you with the necessary skills and mindset to thrive in an ever-changing business environment.

Anticipating and Embracing Industry Shifts

It is crucial for entrepreneurs and business professionals, especially those with a military background, to develop a mindset that allows them to anticipate and embrace industry shifts. In this subchapter, we will explore the importance of staying ahead of the curve, adapting to change, and leveraging your unique skills as a veteran entrepreneur.

As a veteran, you possess a unique set of skills that can be invaluable in navigating industry shifts. Your military experience has taught you to be adaptable, resilient, and resourceful – qualities that are highly sought after in the business world. However, it is essential to recognize that what worked in the military may not always translate directly into the civilian sector. This subchapter will guide you through the process of identifying and leveraging your transferable skills while also developing new ones that are relevant to your chosen industry.

One of the key elements of anticipating and embracing industry shifts is staying informed and being aware of emerging trends and technologies. In the military, you were trained to gather intelligence and assess the battlefield. Apply these skills to your business by regularly conducting market research, monitoring industry news, and attending relevant conferences and seminars. By staying ahead of the curve, you can proactively position yourself and your business to take advantage of emerging opportunities.

In addition to staying informed, it is crucial to foster a mindset that embraces change rather than fearing it. Industry shifts are inevitable, and resisting change can be detrimental to your business's growth and success. Instead, cultivate an attitude of curiosity and a willingness to learn. Seek out new knowledge, explore innovative ideas, and be open to trying new approaches. Remember, adaptability is one of your greatest strengths as a veteran entrepreneur.

Furthermore, it is essential to build a network of like-minded individuals who can support and inspire you on your entrepreneurial journey. Connect with other veteran entrepreneurs, business professionals, and mentors who have successfully navigated industry shifts. By surrounding yourself with individuals who share your values and goals, you can exchange insights, learn from each other's experiences, and collaborate on strategies to thrive in a changing market.

Anticipating and embracing industry shifts is crucial for the success of veteran entrepreneurs. By leveraging your unique skills, staying informed, embracing change, and building a strong network, you can position yourself to not only survive but also thrive in a rapidly evolving business landscape. Remember, as a veteran, you have already faced and overcome numerous challenges – now is the time to apply that warrior mindset to conquer the ever-changing world of business.

Implementing Systems and Processes for Scaling

Scaling your business is a crucial step towards achieving long-term success. However, many entrepreneurs, especially veterans transitioning into the business world, often struggle with the challenges of scaling their ventures effectively. This subchapter will provide you with practical insights and strategies for implementing systems and processes that will enable your business to grow and thrive.

As a veteran entrepreneur, you already possess a unique set of skills and traits that can be leveraged to build a successful business. However, to truly scale your venture and reach new heights of success, you must establish robust systems and processes that can support and sustain growth. These systems and processes will not only streamline your operations but also ensure consistency, efficiency, and effective decision-making.

One of the first steps in implementing systems and processes for scaling is to identify and assess your current operations. This requires a thorough evaluation of your business processes, identifying areas of improvement, and streamlining workflows. By documenting your processes and creating standard operating procedures (SOPs), you can establish a solid foundation for scaling your business.

Another crucial aspect of implementing systems and processes for scaling is to embrace technology and automation. Technology can play a significant role in simplifying tasks, improving efficiency, and enhancing communication within your organization. From project management tools to customer relationship management systems, adopting the right technology can revolutionize your business operations.

Moreover, as a veteran entrepreneur, you understand the importance of discipline and accountability. By instilling a culture of accountability within your organization, you can ensure that everyone is aligned with your business goals and objectives. Regular performance evaluations, goal-setting sessions, and feedback mechanisms can help foster a culture of continuous improvement and drive growth.

Furthermore, as your business expands, it is essential to delegate responsibilities and empower your team members. Delegation not only frees up your time to focus on strategic initiatives but also allows your team to grow and develop their skills. By empowering your employees and providing them with the necessary resources, you create a strong foundation for scaling your business.

Implementing systems and processes for scaling is a critical step for veteran entrepreneurs looking to achieve business success. By evaluating and streamlining your operations, leveraging technology, fostering a culture of accountability, and empowering your team, you can create a scalable framework that will support your business's growth. Remember, scaling your business requires dedication, adaptability, and a warrior mindset.

Continuously Learning and Innovating

In the rapidly evolving landscape of business and entrepreneurship, one thing remains certain - the need for continuous learning and innovation. In the subchapter of "Warrior Mindset, Business Success: A Veteran's Guide to Entrepreneurship" titled "Continuously Learning and Innovating," we explore the importance of staying adaptable, embracing change, and pushing the boundaries of traditional thinking.

For general readers, veterans, business people, and military personnel venturing into the world of entrepreneurship, this subchapter serves as a vital roadmap to success. Drawing upon the unique experiences and perspectives of veteran entrepreneurs, we delve into the mindset required to thrive in the competitive business world.

As a veteran entrepreneur, you already possess a valuable set of skills - discipline, resilience, and a strong work ethic. However, to truly succeed, it is crucial to expand your knowledge and adapt to the ever-changing market dynamics. We discuss the significance of lifelong learning and the various ways to acquire new skills and expertise, whether through formal education, online courses, or industry-specific certifications.

Moreover, we emphasize the importance of constantly seeking innovative solutions to business challenges. By thinking outside the box and embracing change, you can stay ahead of the competition and position your venture for long-term success. We explore case studies of veteran entrepreneurs who have successfully disrupted industries through their innovative approaches and provide practical strategies to foster a culture of innovation within your own business.

Additionally, this subchapter addresses the unique challenges that veteran entrepreneurs may face, such as transitioning from a military mindset to a business mindset and navigating the complexities of the civilian business world. We provide actionable tips and insights to help veterans leverage their military experience and translate their skills into the entrepreneurial realm.

"Continuously Learning and Innovating" serves as a comprehensive guide to equip veteran entrepreneurs with the tools they need to thrive in the business world. By embracing lifelong learning, staying adaptable, and fostering a culture of innovation, you can unlock your full potential and achieve business success. Whether you are a veteran looking to start your own venture or a business professional seeking new strategies, this subchapter is an invaluable resource to fuel your entrepreneurial journey.

Chapter 8: Overcoming Obstacles and Resilience

Dealing with Failure and Setbacks

Failure and setbacks are inevitable in both life and business. They can be disheartening and demoralizing, but they should never be viewed as the end of the road. In fact, failure and setbacks can serve as valuable learning experiences and opportunities for growth. This subchapter will explore strategies for dealing with failure and setbacks, particularly from the perspective of veteran entrepreneurs.

As veterans, we are well-acquainted with adversity and have developed resilience through our military service. This mindset can be applied to the world of entrepreneurship, where failure is often considered a stepping stone to success. It is essential to remember that failure is not a reflection of one's worth or abilities, but rather a chance to learn from mistakes and improve.

The first step in dealing with failure and setbacks is to acknowledge and accept them. It is natural to feel disappointment or frustration, but dwelling on these emotions can hinder progress. Instead, shift your focus to analyzing what went wrong and identifying areas for improvement. This self-reflection is crucial for personal and professional growth.

Next, it is important to maintain a positive mindset. Instead of dwelling on past failures, use them as motivation to push forward. Surround yourself with a support network of like-minded individuals who can provide encouragement and guidance during challenging times. Seek out mentors who have experienced similar setbacks and overcome them. Their wisdom and advice can be invaluable in navigating the path to success.

Another strategy for dealing with failure is to view it as an opportunity for innovation. Failure often provides new perspectives and alternative approaches that can lead to breakthroughs. Embrace a mindset of adaptability and flexibility, allowing you to pivot and adjust your strategies as needed.

Lastly, never give up. Failure is not a permanent state, but rather a temporary setback. The path to success is rarely linear, and setbacks are bound to occur. Embrace these challenges as opportunities for growth, and keep pushing forward with determination and resilience.

Failure and setbacks are a natural part of life and business. As veteran entrepreneurs, we can draw upon our military experience to navigate these challenges with resilience and adaptability. By acknowledging and accepting failure, maintaining a positive mindset, seeking support and guidance, embracing innovation, and never giving up, we can overcome setbacks and achieve success in our entrepreneurial endeavors.

Developing a Growth Mindset

In the pursuit of success, whether in business or any other area of life, having the right mindset is crucial. A growth mindset is an essential quality that can empower individuals to overcome challenges, adapt to new situations, and ultimately achieve their goals. In this subchapter, we will explore the concept of developing a growth mindset and how it can benefit veterans, business people, military personnel, and particularly those in the niche of the veteran entrepreneur.

A growth mindset is the belief that one's abilities can be developed through dedication, effort, and perseverance. It is the understanding that intelligence and talent are not fixed traits, but rather qualities that can be cultivated and expanded. This mindset encourages individuals to embrace challenges, view failures as opportunities for growth, and seek out learning experiences.

For veterans transitioning into the business world, developing a growth mindset can be especially beneficial. The military instills values such as discipline, resilience, and adaptability, which are all valuable traits for entrepreneurship. By adopting a growth mindset, veterans can leverage these qualities to navigate the challenges of starting and running their own businesses.

In the world of business, setbacks are inevitable. However, with a growth mindset, individuals are more likely to view these setbacks as temporary hurdles rather than insurmountable obstacles. They understand that failure is not a reflection of their worth or abilities, but rather an opportunity to learn, adapt, and improve. This mindset allows them to bounce back stronger and more determined than ever before.

Moreover, a growth mindset encourages individuals to continuously seek out new knowledge and skills. Veterans, with their natural inclination towards lifelong learning, can capitalize on this mindset to stay ahead in the ever-evolving business landscape. By embracing new technologies, trends, and ideas, veteran entrepreneurs can remain agile and innovative, giving them a competitive edge in the marketplace.

To cultivate a growth mindset, individuals must be willing to step outside of their comfort zones, take calculated risks, and persist in the face of adversity. It requires a shift in perspective, from a fixed mindset that believes abilities are predetermined, to a growth mindset that sees the potential for continuous improvement.

Developing a growth mindset is crucial for veterans, business people, military personnel, and especially for those in the niche of the veteran entrepreneur. By embracing challenges, viewing failures as opportunities, and seeking out continuous learning, individuals can unlock their full potential and achieve extraordinary success in the world of business.

Learning from Mistakes and Moving Forward

Mistakes are an inevitable part of life, and the path to success is often paved with failures. In the journey of entrepreneurship, every businessperson, military personnel, and veteran will encounter setbacks and make errors. However, what sets successful individuals apart is their ability to learn from these mistakes and use them as stepping stones to move forward.

As a veteran entrepreneur, you possess a unique set of skills and experiences that can be leveraged to thrive in the business world. Your military training has instilled in you resilience, discipline, and adaptability, qualities that are invaluable in the realm of entrepreneurship. Nevertheless, it is essential to recognize that mistakes will occur, and embracing them as learning opportunities is crucial.

One of the first steps in learning from mistakes is to acknowledge them openly and honestly. Avoiding or denying errors will only impede your growth. Instead, confront the mistake head-on, analyze the root causes, and identify the lessons to be learned. By doing so, you will gain valuable insights that can prevent similar mistakes in the future.

Another vital aspect of learning from mistakes is to adopt a growth mindset. Understand that failure is not an end but a stepping stone toward improvement. Embrace the mindset that mistakes are an essential part of the learning process and that each misstep brings you closer to success. By reframing failures as opportunities for growth, you will be more motivated to persevere and push through challenges.

Additionally, seek feedback and advice from mentors, fellow veterans, and businesspeople who have faced similar situations. Their perspectives and insights can provide alternative viewpoints and help you learn from their experiences. Networking within the veteran entrepreneur community is a valuable resource for support and guidance.

Moving forward, it is crucial to apply the lessons learned from mistakes to your business strategies. Develop a continuous improvement mindset and make adjustments based on your newfound knowledge. Implementing changes and refining your approach will enable you to adapt and stay ahead in the ever-evolving business landscape.

Learning from mistakes is an essential skill for any entrepreneur, particularly for veteran entrepreneurs. Embrace failure as a necessary part of the journey, confront mistakes openly, and approach them with a growth mindset. Seek feedback, learn from others, and apply the lessons to continuously improve your business strategies. By cultivating this mindset, you will not only overcome obstacles but also thrive in your entrepreneurial endeavors. Remember, success often lies on the other side of failure.

Seeking Support and Mentorship

In the entrepreneurial journey, seeking support and mentorship can make all the difference between success and failure. This holds true for individuals from all walks of life, but it holds special significance for veterans transitioning into entrepreneurship. As a veteran entrepreneur, you possess a unique set of skills and experiences that can propel you towards business success. However, to fully leverage your potential, it is crucial to seek support and mentorship from those who have walked the path before you.

One of the primary challenges faced by veteran entrepreneurs is the transition from a structured military environment to the dynamic world of business. This transition can be overwhelming, as you navigate through unfamiliar territory. This is where seeking support becomes crucial. Connecting with fellow veterans who have successfully made the leap into entrepreneurship can provide invaluable guidance and advice. They understand the challenges you face and can offer insights on how to overcome them. Joining veteran entrepreneur networks or attending industry-specific events can help you build a support system and foster meaningful connections.

Mentorship is another powerful tool for veteran entrepreneurs. A mentor can provide personalized guidance, share their knowledge and experiences, and help you avoid common pitfalls. Seek out mentors who have not only excelled in the business world but also have a deep understanding of the military background. They can help you bridge the gap between your military service and entrepreneurial aspirations. A mentor can also provide emotional support, helping you stay focused and motivated during challenging times.

There are various avenues to find mentors, such as industry associations, business incubators, and online platforms. Additionally, consider reaching out to successful veteran entrepreneurs who inspire you. Many of them are willing to give back and support fellow veterans on their entrepreneurial journey.

Remember, seeking support and mentorship is not a sign of weakness, but rather a testament to your commitment to personal and professional growth. It is essential to surround yourself with individuals who believe in your potential and can offer guidance when you encounter roadblocks.

Seeking support and mentorship is vital for veteran entrepreneurs. By connecting with fellow veterans and finding mentors who understand your unique background, you gain access to a wealth of knowledge and support. Embrace the power of community and tap into the wisdom of those who have already paved the way. With the right support system and mentorship, you can navigate the challenges of entrepreneurship with confidence and achieve remarkable success.

Balancing Work and Personal Life

Finding a balance between work and personal life can be a challenging task. This is particularly true for individuals who have served in the military and are now venturing into the world of entrepreneurship. However, with the right mindset and strategies, achieving this balance is not only possible but also crucial for long-term success.

For veteran entrepreneurs, the transition from military life to running their own business can be overwhelming. The discipline and dedication instilled in them during their service can sometimes lead to an all-consuming work mentality. This can strain personal relationships, cause burnout, and ultimately hinder business growth. Therefore, finding ways to strike a healthy balance becomes essential.

One effective approach is to establish clear boundaries between work and personal life. Set specific working hours and try to stick to them as much as possible. This will ensure that you have dedicated time for family, friends, and personal activities. Avoid bringing work-related stress into your personal life by creating a physical and mental separation between the two spheres.

Another important aspect of balancing work and personal life is prioritization. As a veteran entrepreneur, it is easy to become consumed by the demands of your business. However, it is crucial to identify the most important tasks and allocate time accordingly. This will prevent you from feeling overwhelmed and allow you to maintain a sense of control over your personal life.

Additionally, learning to delegate and ask for help is vital for achieving a healthy work-life balance. Many veterans possess a strong sense of self-reliance, but running a successful business requires collaboration and support. Surround yourself with a reliable team or seek mentorship from fellow entrepreneurs who can share their experiences and insights.

Moreover, taking care of your physical and mental well-being is essential for maintaining a healthy work-life balance. Engaging in regular exercise, practicing mindfulness or meditation, and setting aside time for hobbies and relaxation are all crucial for recharging and avoiding burnout.

Finding a balance between work and personal life is an ongoing process that requires constant evaluation and adaptation. As a veteran entrepreneur, it is important to remember that success in business should not come at the expense of your personal happiness and well-being. By establishing boundaries, prioritizing tasks, seeking support, and prioritizing self-care, you can achieve the delicate balance that allows you to thrive both professionally and personally.

Prioritizing Health and Well-being

It's easy to get caught up in the hustle and bustle of running a business. However, as a veteran entrepreneur, it is crucial to prioritize your health and well-being to achieve long-term success. This subchapter explores the importance of self-care, physical fitness, and mental resilience in the journey of a veteran entrepreneur.

As veterans, we are familiar with the concept of putting others before ourselves. However, when it comes to entrepreneurship, it is essential to remember that we cannot pour from an empty cup. Taking care of our physical and mental health should be at the top of our priority list. By investing time and effort into self-care, we can ensure we have the energy and focus needed to tackle the challenges that come with running a business.

One aspect of self-care is maintaining physical fitness. Regular exercise not only promotes good health but also increases productivity and mental clarity. Whether it's hitting the gym, going for a run, or practicing yoga, finding an exercise routine that suits your preferences and schedule is vital. By incorporating physical activity into your daily routine, you will not only feel better physically but also experience increased mental resilience, allowing you to handle stress and setbacks with ease.

Mental resilience is another crucial aspect of prioritizing health and well-being as a veteran entrepreneur. Building mental strength and developing coping mechanisms for stress and pressure can significantly impact your ability to navigate the challenges of entrepreneurship. This involves embracing a growth mindset, practicing mindfulness and meditation, and seeking support from mentors, peers, or mental health professionals when needed.

In addition to self-care, it is essential to create a work-life balance. Being an entrepreneur is demanding, but it should not come at the cost of your personal relationships or overall well-being. Setting boundaries and making time for family, friends, and hobbies is crucial for maintaining a healthy and fulfilling life.

Prioritizing health and well-being is a vital component of being a successful veteran entrepreneur. By taking care of ourselves physically and mentally, we can ensure we have the resilience, focus, and energy needed to overcome challenges and achieve long-term success. Remember, your well-being is not a luxury; it is a necessity for your business and personal growth.

Managing Stress and Burnout

Stress and burnout are all too common. This is especially true for veterans who have transitioned from the military to the business world. However, with the right strategies and mindset, it is possible to effectively manage stress and avoid burnout while building a successful business.

Recognizing the signs of stress and burnout is the first step towards managing them. As a veteran entrepreneur, you may be accustomed to pushing through challenges and ignoring the toll it takes on your mental and physical well-being. It is important to remember that self-care is not a sign of weakness but a necessary part of maintaining a healthy and sustainable business.

One effective way to manage stress is through the practice of mindfulness. Mindfulness involves being fully present in the moment and observing thoughts and emotions without judgment. By incorporating mindfulness techniques into your daily routine, such as meditation or deep breathing exercises, you can reduce stress levels and improve your overall well-being.

Another crucial aspect of managing stress and burnout is maintaining a healthy work-life balance. As a veteran entrepreneur, it can be tempting to devote all your time and energy to your business. However, neglecting other areas of your life can lead to burnout and negatively impact your mental health. Set clear boundaries between work and personal life, and make time for activities that bring you joy and relaxation.

Building a support network is also essential for managing stress and burnout. Surround yourself with like-minded individuals who understand the unique challenges of being a veteran entrepreneur. Seek out mentorship opportunities, join industry-related groups, and participate in networking events. A strong support system can provide valuable advice, encouragement, and a sense of camaraderie during difficult times.

Finally, it is crucial to regularly assess and reassess your goals and priorities. As a veteran, you may have a natural inclination to push yourself to the limit. However, it is important to remember that success is not solely measured by financial achievements but also by personal well-being and fulfillment. Take the time to reflect on your values and ensure that your business aligns with them.

Managing stress and avoiding burnout is a continuous process that requires self-awareness, self-care, and a commitment to personal well-being. By implementing these strategies and maintaining a warrior mindset, you can navigate the challenges of entrepreneurship while preserving your mental and physical health. Remember, your well-being is the foundation for long-term business success.

Nurturing Relationships and Finding Support

One of the most critical aspects of achieving success as a veteran entrepreneur is nurturing relationships and finding a solid support network. As you embark on your journey as a business owner, it is important to recognize that you cannot do it all alone. Building and maintaining strong connections with others not only provides you with valuable support but also opens doors to new opportunities and collaborations.

For veterans, having a network of fellow veterans who are also entrepreneurs can be particularly beneficial. These individuals understand the unique challenges and experiences that come with transitioning from military service to the business world. They can offer guidance, share resources, and provide a sense of camaraderie that is unparalleled.

To nurture relationships effectively, it is crucial to be proactive and intentional. Attend networking events, join veteran entrepreneur organizations, and reach out to fellow veterans in your industry. Engaging in these activities will not only help you expand your network but also allow you to learn from others who have walked a similar path.

In addition to veteran-specific connections, it is vital to cultivate relationships with individuals from diverse backgrounds and industries. Collaborating with professionals outside of the military sphere can provide fresh perspectives and unique insights. Seek out mentors, advisors, and business coaches who can offer guidance and expertise in areas where you may lack experience.

Finding support also extends beyond personal connections. Building a team of trusted advisors, such as accountants, lawyers, and marketing experts, is essential for navigating the complexities of running a business. These professionals can provide valuable guidance and help you make informed decisions that align with your long-term goals.

Remember that relationships are not one-sided; they require effort and reciprocity. Be willing to offer support and assistance to others in your network whenever possible. By providing value and cultivating a reputation as a reliable and helpful individual, you will strengthen your relationships and build a network that is eager to support you in return.

Ultimately, nurturing relationships and finding support as a veteran entrepreneur is about creating a community of like-minded individuals who are dedicated to helping each other succeed. By actively seeking out these connections and fostering meaningful relationships, you will not only enhance your chances of business success but also find a sense of fulfillment and support in your entrepreneurial journey.

Conclusion: The Warrior Entrepreneur's Journey to Success

The path to success is often filled with challenges and uncertainties. For veterans transitioning into entrepreneurship, this journey can be even more daunting. However, armed with the warrior mindset and the unique skills acquired through military service, the veteran entrepreneur possesses a powerful advantage.

In this book, "Warrior Mindset: A Veteran's Guide to Entrepreneurship and Business" we have explored the essential elements that pave the way for a successful transition from military service to entrepreneurship. From harnessing the warrior mindset to leveraging military experience, we have provided practical strategies and insights to guide veterans on their path to business success.

Throughout the chapters, we have emphasized the importance of adaptability and resilience. The ability to adapt to changing circumstances and overcome obstacles is inherent in the warrior spirit. By embracing these qualities, veterans can navigate the unpredictable terrain of entrepreneurship and emerge victorious.

We have also highlighted the significance of leveraging military experience. The skills acquired in the military, such as leadership, teamwork, discipline, and problem-solving, are invaluable assets in the business world. By harnessing these skills and translating them into the entrepreneurial context, veterans can gain a competitive edge and excel in their ventures.

Furthermore, we have emphasized the importance of building a strong support network. Veterans possess a unique bond, and by connecting with fellow veterans, business people, and military personnel, they can create a community that provides guidance, inspiration, and collaboration. This network can help overcome challenges and provide the necessary support to thrive in the entrepreneurial world.

the journey to success for the veteran entrepreneur is a testament to the indomitable spirit and resilience of our military personnel. By embracing the warrior mindset, leveraging military experience, and building a strong support network, veterans can overcome the obstacles they encounter and achieve their entrepreneurial goals.

This book serves as a guide and a source of inspiration for veterans, business people, and military personnel alike. It is our hope that through the lessons and insights shared within these pages, we can empower and support those embarking on the warrior entrepreneur's journey to success. Remember, the warrior within you is equipped to conquer any challenge and seize the opportunities that await in the world of business.

ABOUT THE AUTHOR

DR. JOSE A. MENDEZ is not your average author; he's a man of unwavering faith, a loving husband, Air Force veteran, father, and ardent dog lover, especially his service dog Knox, a Black Labrador who is his faithful companion. Dr. Mendez is a multifaceted professional whose journey through life has been as diverse as it is inspiring.

Born and raised in the vibrant West Coast of Puerto Rico, Dr. Mendez's early life was deeply influenced by his cultural heritage and the stunning natural beauty of his island home. It's here that he developed a lifelong passion for outdoor adventures, particularly scuba diving, kayaking, and fishing. These pursuits, fueled by his deep respect for nature, have not only provided him with a sense of serenity but have also taught him valuable lessons in patience, perseverance, and the importance of harmonizing with the environment.

Dr. Mendez's commitment to faith is the result of a life-changing experience; and has been a guiding force throughout his life. As a man deeply rooted in Christian principles, he has applied his unwavering belief system to every facet of his personal and professional life. His faith is the cornerstone upon which he has built his career as an educator, author, and entrepreneur.

With an impressive educational background, Dr. Mendez holds a Doctorate in Business Administration with specializations in Entrepreneurship and Business Management. He has also earned a Master's degree in Business Administration with a focus on Project Management and Quality Control, showcasing his commitment to excellence and precision in every endeavor.

In addition to his business acumen, Dr. Mendez has delved into the world of intelligence studies. He holds a Master's degree in Intelligence Studies, bringing a unique perspective to his work and further demonstrating his dedication to continuous learning and understanding complex systems.

Dr. Mendez's journey has also been marked by his dedication to service. He is a military veteran, having proudly served his country. His time in the military has not only enriched his character but has instilled in him a profound sense of duty, discipline, and leadership. As well as giving him a deep understanding of the best and worst that humanity has to offer.

Beyond his academic and professional achievements, Dr. Mendez is a devoted family man. As a loving husband and father, he cherishes the bonds he shares with his loved ones and draws inspiration from their unwavering support.

His love for dogs is another facet of his life that brings joy and warmth to his days. He understands the profound loyalty and companionship that these four-legged friends offer and has embraced them as cherished members of his family.

In his latest work, "Warrior Mindset: A Veteran's Guide to Entrepreneurship and Business," Dr. Mendez combines his expertise in business with his understanding of the military warrior mindset, to offer readers a unique perspective on how to build successful, purpose-driven businesses that reflect Christian values.

Dr. Jose A. Mendez's life story is one of faith, adventure, dedication, and love. Through his journey, he has not only achieved academic and professional excellence but has also found fulfillment in his faith, his life experience, his family, and his love for what life has to offer. His writing reflects the wisdom and passion that have shaped his remarkable life, offering readers a glimpse into the mind and heart of a man who believes that faith, business, and life can coexist in perfect harmony.

Don't miss out!

Visit the website below and you can sign up to receive emails whenever Dr. Jose A. Mendez publishes a new book. There's no charge and no obligation.

https://books2read.com/r/B-A-UGHEB-DFHYC

BOOKS 2 READ

Connecting independent readers to independent writers.

About the Author

Dr. Jose A. Mendez is not your average author; he's a man of unwavering faith, a loving husband, Air Force veteran, father, and ardent dog lover, especially his service dog Knox, a Black Labrador who is his faithful companion. Dr. Mendez is a multifaceted professional whose journey through life has been as diverse as it is inspiring.

Born and raised in the vibrant West Coast of Puerto Rico, Dr. Mendez's early life was deeply influenced by his cultural heritage and the stunning natural beauty of his island home. It's here that he developed a lifelong passion for outdoor adventures, particularly scuba diving, kayaking, and fishing.

Dr. Mendez's commitment to faith is the result of a life-changing experience; and has been a guiding force throughout his life. As a man deeply rooted in Christian principles, he has applied his unwavering belief system to every facet of his personal and professional life. His faith is the cornerstone upon which he has built his career as an educator, author, and entrepreneur.

With an impressive educational background, Dr. Mendez holds a Doctorate in Business Administration with specializations in Entrepreneurship and Business Management. He has also earned a Master's degree in Business Administration with a focus on Project Management and Quality Control, showcasing his commitment to excellence and precision in every endeavor.

Dr. Mendez's journey has also been marked by his dedication to service. He is a military veteran, having proudly served his country. His time in the military has not only enriched his character but has instilled in him a profound sense of duty, discipline, and leadership. As well as giving him a deep understanding of the best and worst that humanity has to offer.

Beyond his academic and professional achievements, Dr. Mendez is a devoted family man. As a loving husband and father, he cherishes the bonds he shares with his loved ones and draws inspiration from their unwavering support.

In his latest work, "Warrior Mindset: A Veteran's Guide to Entrepreneurship and Business," Dr. Mendez combines his expertise in business with his understanding of the military warrior mindset, to offer readers a unique perspective on how to build successful, purpose-driven businesses.

About the Publisher

At Christian Cross Publishing, we believe in the power of stories. Our vision is aimed at empowering faith through literature. We strive to illuminate hearts and minds with inspirational words that embody the timeless message of love, hope, and redemption.

Read more at https://christiancrosspublishing.com/.

www.ingramcontent.com/pod-product-compliance
Lightning Source LLC
Chambersburg PA
CBHW031429150726
47989CB00002B/860